BORROWED HEART

HEART

The True Story

GLEN W. PARK

BORROWED HEART

The True Story

By Glen W. Park
Published by Vision, Inc.
Publications Division
P. O. Box 17181
Salt Lake City, UT 84117

© Copyright 2004-2013 By Glen W. Park, Salt Lake City, Utah. All Rights Reserved. No part of this publication may be used or reproduced in any manner, stored in a retrieval system now known or to be invented, or transmitted in any form or by any means—printed, electronic, digital, photocopy, recording, or any other—except for brief quotations in printed reviews, without the prior written permission of the author.

ISBN: 978-1484805060

Library of Congress Control Number: 2013942854

Cover Design by Anne P. Inouye.

Cover Image by Monia33 through Dreamstime. Used by permission.

Printed in the United States of America.

DEDICATION

To my wife, Dianne, the love of my lives. Also to my children and grandchildren who have brought me so much joy and fun.

CONTENTS

ACKNOWLEDGMENTS

I wish to acknowledge the inspiration and assistance of many in the commencement and completion of this book.

The comfort, inspiration and impressions of the Spirit during numerous difficult times in my life assured me of the Lord's love and motivated/lead me to seek additional knowledge and faith, and to strive to be more obedient and worthy. This effort brought even more inspiration and a greater testimony of His existence and love.

My parents, brothers and sisters encouraged me to seek after good things and provided me opportunities to achieve and learn. The loss of my parents while I was young spurred me to search for answers to spiritual questions. The answers to those questions, received through the Holy Ghost, brought me peace and an increased desire to be faithful and obedient to the Lord.

My dear wife, Dianne, and my desire to share eternity with her, have been a continuing motivation to fight to live. Together, we have sought to turn our will over to His will in order to please Him and to be worthy of His great blessings.

My children have been a source of joy and motivation for me to live and strive to be better, to be able to share eternity with them.

My deep gratitude goes to my doctors, transplant coordinators, nurses and all others at the University of Utah Heart Transplant Department. I thank a wonderful donor and her family for making it possible for me to receive this Borrowed Heart, that saved my life.

I appreciate the assistance of my son, Craig, and my daughter-in-law, Melissa, in helping me to review this book. I thank my daughter, Anne, for a superb job on the production of the cover of this book.

The Lord's miraculous preservation, restoration and extension of my life are wonderful beyond expression. These miracles and the lessons and growth they afforded, inspired me to complete this work in the hope that those who read it will be comforted and inspired.

FOREWARD

It seems that everyone's life has many trials—some very serious. In the midst of these trials, most people have numerous opportunities for spiritual experiences and growth. This is the story of mine.

Many around me who have been closely involved in my life and many others who have become acquainted with many of my seriously difficult and wonderfully spiritual experiences have encouraged me—even repeatedly pushed me—to write and publish the more significant of my experiences. It has been their belief, and it has become mine as well, that those who read this book will find some similarities with their own lives. But there will also be numerous differences that will serve to inform and inspire the reader to view life and that which follows mortality in a positive light, and trials as opportunities. Moreover, it is my sincere hope that this account will lift and encourage all to "hang in there" and to seek to better understand the spiritual elements of mortal life and to draw nearer to God and to the immense power and blessings of a close relationship with Him. He loves each of His spirit children. Therefore, many similar spiritual experiences can be available to all who earnestly seek to draw near to Him and to become more like Him.

CHAPTER ONE

LOSING DAD

"Something has happened to your father.
He is at the Cottonwood Hospital. I think you
should go there immediately."

I know of no one who's heart has stopped more than mine. Undoubtedly, there have been others whose hearts have stopped more, but I am not acquainted with them. The important thing, however, is that my heart has re-started as many times as it has stopped. The stops, the starts and many happenings before, in between and since are what I will discuss herein. In this book, I relate numerous difficult and many special experiences in my life, as I remember them. Most of the difficult times came in my experiencing the loss of my parents while only a teenager or in my own serious health problems that came later in my life. The special ones generally came in wonderful times with my family or through spiritual experiences given me by the Lord—often during or following my most difficult times.

The general rule is that when people experience serious trials in life, they generally respond in one of two ways: (1) they humble themselves before God and seek His assistance, strength and comfort; or (2) they become angry at the Lord for "causing" such misery and they justify themselves in turning away from Him.

Having seen both of these responses and understanding what it takes and how it blesses one to follow the first path, I determined to write this book in the hope that many readers will be encouraged to seek the Lord before and during times of trial.

The Lord has been very kind to me, extending numerous tender mercies throughout my life. When still less than ten years of age, I prayed to see if He really was aware of me. I believed that God was real, and whenever I prayed to Him with full purpose of heart, I fully expected him to hear and to answer. That may sound presumptuous, but there was nothing cocky about it. I simply had a personal witness that I was one of His spirit sons and He loved me.

His answers came with quiet assurance to my heart. I knew then that God, my Father in Heaven, was real. I felt certain He knew and loved me. That assurance stayed with me from that time on, becoming only deeper and stronger as the Lord continued to give me answers and assurances throughout my life. Please note that the fact that He answered my prayers does not mean He always said, "Yes."

I was quite athletic, loved nearly all sports and was very active in playing them as well as in playing other games with family and friends. Sometime near the age of twelve, I also spent more time reading scriptures than the average boy. As I read, I felt a witness that the scriptures were true, that God lives, that He is mindful of me and that He hears my prayers. I came to know He still communicates with His chosen representatives on Earth—prophets—and he also communicates with individuals according to their faith. Those other individuals included me.

Throughout my teen years, I continued to receive answers to my prayers and quiet reassurances of God's existence and of the truthfulness of the teachings of His prophets and of the scriptures.

When I was seventeen years old and a senior in high school, I went one Saturday morning to a nearby town, driving my 1955 Chevrolet to meet my father at a dealer's repair department. The mechanic checked something on my car, and then I left to meet my father at the two acres my brother, Ray, owned. Other brothers and I were going to help Ray do some work there.

After being there a short time, Dad said he was leaving to go home and get some things done there. The last time I ever saw him alive—although I did not know it at the time—was as he walked away from us, there on my brother's property. I still have very clearly in my mind's eye Dad walking away, waving goodbye after we called out "Goodbye" to him.

Some hours later, I left Ray's land and drove east along 4100 South toward home. Somewhere nearly half-way home, I passed my neighbor, Gerald Little, driving in the opposite direction. For whatever reason, I noticed who it was, and felt that I should pull over to the side of the road. I did so, and he stopped, made a U-turn, and pulled up behind my car. He came up to my car and said, "Something has happened to your father. He is at the Cottonwood Hospital. I think you should go there immediately."

I asked, "What happened? Is he okay?"

"I don't know. I think it's pretty serious," he answered.

I thanked him and took off for the hospital. While I drove, I uttered a sincere prayer that my dad would be okay. It was a sincere, heart-felt prayer to a God I knew was there and would hear it.

The answer came. I knew the answer was not self-sent for it was the exact opposite of that for which I had prayed. The quiet feeling came over me that Dad was dead. I knew it. I knew it not because it was what I wanted but in spite of what I wanted. The significant thing to me was that the Lord was caring enough of me that He would so communicate with me. He let me know that He knew me, that He loved me and cared enough for me that He would answer my prayer and tell me the truth concerning my father.

Some people receive such an answer and become angry with God for giving an answer that is not the result they have sought— that He answered "No." God is not a waiter, who takes our order and quickly delivers what we have requested. It has been wisely stated that if God really wanted to punish or curse us, He would give us everything we ask for.

Hundreds of times throughout my life, I have received answers from the Lord—inspiration, assurances, direction and comfort. I received clear impressions that would forewarn me of things to come and of actions I should and should not take. I quickly learned to rely, without question, upon those impressions that I know come from the Lord through the Spirit.

The drive to the hospital seemed to take hours, although it actually was only twenty minutes or so. I arrived at the Cottonwood Hospital and rushed into Emergency. After telling the receptionist who I was and for whom I had come, I was met by a doctor who asked me several questions about the last time I saw my dad. He then told me that Dad had suffered a major heart attack and had not survived.

He indicated where other members of my family were and I went into the room where my mother and brother, John, were waiting. We hugged and grieved together as John recounted his having found Dad in the backyard when he went to call him in for lunch. He had unsuccessfully tried to resuscitate him.

Mom was in shock. I guess we all were. That day and the next, we went through the process of grieving and planning Dad's funeral and burial. I just seemed to be in a daze. Several memories stand out very distinctly. None of us were prepared for this loss. Each brother and sister was seeking to comfort the others. They all seemed concerned about me, the youngest in the family. A few of my high school friends came to visit me. They really did not know what to say, except "We're so sorry. Is there anything we can do?"

There really was nothing they could do. And yet, they were actually already doing it. Their coming and showing they cared was all they could do and all they needed to do. I have remembered that all my life. When I have tried to give comfort to others over their loss of a loved one, I have recalled that experience of my own. My being with them and letting them know of my concern and love is about all I can do. There are definitely times when I can speak comforting words of consolation, express spiritual truths and try to bring the Spirit into the conversation. These extras do add to my being there, and I try to do that every time I seek to comfort those who I know are sorrowing from the loss of a loved one. They feel the Spirit, and so do I. But my merely being there brings comfort and lifts them.

Mom and all of the children stood together at the viewing on Monday evening and Tuesday morning, prior to the funeral. My sister, Lois, stood next to Mom, followed by the rest of us, in order of birth. So I was last, standing next to my brother, John. I remember how empty our house felt that night after the funeral. It took months for that emptiness to leave to any real extent.

CHAPTER TWO

LOSING MOM

"What am I supposed to do? My mother is lying on the floor . . ."

A few days after Dad's funeral, Mom and I were together in our home. As we were talking, I broke down, crying. Immediately, Mom broke down into tears as well. I felt the need to comfort her. It took some time to do so. I learned something from that experience. I saw that I needed to be strong for her sake. I needed to make sure that I did not bring her down by breaking down myself. So I made certain from that time on to grieve on my own, whenever possible, when I was alone. I worked hard from then on to support and give strength and comfort to my mother.

The next time the Lord gave me a distinctly clear impression was about three and a half months later. I came home from school to find the back door of our home locked from the inside. The lock was one that required a certain type of skeleton key to lock and unlock it. Not only was it locked, but the key was still in the lock from the inside. The keyhole in this type of lock was open clear through such that one could look from either side through the lock to the other side of the door. So, when a key was in the lock, the end of it could be seen in the lock from the other side.

I knocked on the door again and again. There was no answer. After knocking numerous times, I went to the front door, which was locked as it always was. I did not have a key to that door. I walked around to another room's window and before looking into it—just in case Mom was dressing therein—I knocked on the window and waited about a minute. Then I knocked again and looked into the room. It was empty. Now, I was very worried.

I ran back to the locked rear door and worked at pushing the key out of the lock. Finally, after a long time, the key fell out of the lock. I put my key in, turned it, and opened the door. I ran into the kitchen. There on the floor, lay my mom. She was conscious, looking up at me. I knelt down and held her to me. I asked her if she was okay. She could not talk. She tried to smile, but could not control her facial muscles. I took her hand, and she squeezed mine. I told her I was going to call for an ambulance and would be right back.

I ran to the telephone, called the operator and told her that I needed an ambulance. She answered, "That is not what I do."

I cried out, "What am I supposed to do? My mother is lying on the floor and I don't have a telephone number to call for an ambulance." (This was before "911" had been instituted.)

The operator responded, "Just a minute."

After some time, a person came on the line, took our address and circumstances and said he was sending an ambulance. "It will be there in a few minutes."

I returned to Mom and lay down next to her. I held her hand and told her that everything was going to be okay. It seemed like forever before there was a loud knock at the door. I ran to open it to the emergency responders there. One asked me several questions as the other examined Mom. They lifted her onto a gurney and took her to the ambulance. They told me to what hospital they would be taking her and that I should drive there in my own car. I quickly called some of my brothers and sisters, told them what had happened, and then drove to the hospital.

Mom had suffered a severe stroke and was paralyzed on one side of her body. She could not speak. All of us took turns spending time with her and talking to her. It was so hard to see her lying there on the hospital bed, unable to speak or do anything for herself. We spent the next three days taking turns resting at home, being in the waiting room or spending time in her room with her.

On Saturday morning, January 25, 1969, just over three and a half months after my father's death, I was sitting in the waiting area just outside of Mom's hospital room. I looked up at the clock, and instead of seeing the time of morning it actually was, I saw on the clock's face a specific time in the afternoon—at least I saw it in my mind's eye. I fought the notion but felt certain that Mom would die this afternoon. I prayed so hard that this would not be so. But the Spirit whispered otherwise. Again, I had received an answer I knew was not from myself, for it certainly was not of my choosing. I also knew the real Source of the answer.

That afternoon, Mom passed away. Although I was devastated, I did receive comfort that in this time of such great sorrow and loss, the Lord was again mindful of me, and had communicated to me in advance what was to come. Although I did not want that result, I was comforted to know that the Lord knew me and had sent His Spirit to communicate with me. Again it was confirmed to me that God lives, that He knows me and cares about me.

Despite the Spirit's inspiration and the comfort He gave me, I was devastated. But I was not angry with the Lord. I had been so close to Mom. She had been so good and kind to me. Since my next-youngest sibling, John, was more than six years older than I, my days as a little boy were spent at home with Mom while my brothers and sisters were either at school or work. I had indeed been blessed with a great deal of time—years—mostly alone with my angel mother.

She read to me until I learned how to read. Then she read with me. She taught me so many things. She spent hours every day with me. But she also let me have alone time to do things myself. I learned very early in life to entertain myself and to be content without being entertained by television or other people. It was a great thing to learn, for it enabled me to be content even when I was alone and without any obvious entertainment. I am convinced this helped me to accomplish much more than I otherwise would have in life, for I have not always needed to be doing something fun, or talking with, others to be happy. In addition to that, I learned how much Mom loved and cared for me. She would stay up evenings with me and we would do many different activities together. We played cards and other games. We talked about many things. She answered my questions.

When I was four years old, I grew interested in numbers and addition. Almost every night, I would ask Mom to give me numbers to add. She would ask something like: What is 17 plus 15, plus 9, plus 22, plus 7, plus 19? I quickly added them in my head and gave her the answer. I insisted that she give me many different sets of numbers to add. She never seemed to tire of doing so, although looking back upon the experience, it must have been very monotonous for her. But she never let me know if it was. A thought only recently occurred to me. I just always assumed that Mom knew the answer and was checking to see that I was right. Maybe she was, and maybe she wasn't. It doesn't matter now. Her doing this at my request was fun for me. It helped me a great deal, and it showed me her unfaltering love for me.

When I went to church or some church activity with my brothers John and Ray, their friends would come up to me and give me numbers to add. I would give them the sum, and every time they seemed to be amazed.

Mom and I went shopping together. We talked about God and shared a great relationship during my formative years. I will forever be grateful to her. I am also grateful to my dad for working so hard so Mom could be a stay-at-home mom for me, my brothers and sisters.

But now she was gone. With both Mom and Dad gone, much of my world also seemed to be gone.

About five weeks after my mother died, I was called to the principal's office and informed that I was first in my graduating class of over 700 students. I was excited until I arrived home. I went into the empty house, walked into the empty, dark kitchen. I called out, "So what!" Neither Dad nor Mom was there to share in that accomplishment. Much of the joy and excitement that might have been there just wasn't. I called some of my siblings. They praised me for that accomplishment. It was nice, but not quite the same.

CHAPTER THREE

LIFE ON MY OWN

"I won't be here forever to help you."

Nearly two months prior to his death, Dad had taken me outside and walked around our house and yard with me. He showed me where water lines ran, talked to me about equipment and landscaping. He reviewed the process of shutting things off in preparation for winter, and then turning them back on in the spring. He then told me that for many years, he had not thought college was particularly necessary. "But," he explained, "I see now that it is very important. As well as you have done in school, you should go to college. That way, you will be able to get a better job than you would otherwise. I want you to get through college as fast as you can. I won't be here forever to help you."

Now, following Mom's death, I remembered Dad's counsel to me. Indeed, he would not be here to help me. I still took his advice seriously. But I had something else to work out in my mind. I had received Dad's serious, prescient counsel. I also felt that the Lord would want me to serve a mission for Him. Serving a mission would postpone finishing my college education—or so I thought—by two years. I was determined not to put anything before the Lord in my life. But I also wanted to respect my father's wishes and counsel. How to do so was now the focus of serious thought, reflection and prayer. I did not share with anyone what I was pondering, except the Lord. I poured my heart out to Him for answers. The impression came to me to get my patriarchal blessing. So I went to my Bishop and received a recommend for a blessing. I still told no one what I was trying to reconcile. Even when I met alone with the Patriarch, I said nothing about this situation. After a very brief talk, he placed his hands on my head and pronounced my patriarchal blessing. This occurred on April 20, 1969, the eighteenth birthday of the person who would later become my wife.

In that blessing, the Patriarch told me a lot of wonderful and important things. Those most relevant to this account are: (1) that my parents are able to look down on me as I round out my life, and that I would bring honor and joy to them by the life I would lead; and (2) that I would serve a mission.

The first was another witness to me that God lives and that there is a spirit life after mortality. I have already published a book about that post-mortal life entitled *Our Next Life: A View Into The Spirit World*. My parents now dwell there. They continue to live, albeit separated from their mortal bodies. They are still concerned about me and still love me. They continue to want the best for me and even thrill in my worthy accomplishments.

The second was also a witness to me that God lives and had heard my sincere and serious prayers about serving a mission. He had chosen an unmistakable way to give me His answer. There were multiple paragraphs in my blessing about the mission I would serve.

In The Doctrine and Covenants, Section 6, the Lord speaks peace to Oliver Cowdery in answer to Oliver's prayers. Later, when

Oliver is requesting an additional blessing, the Lord answers, referring to His previous answer to Oliver.

> Verily, verily, I say unto you, if you desire a further witness, cast your mind upon the night that you cried unto me in your heart, that you might know concerning the truth of these things.
>
> Did I not speak peace to your mind concerning the matter? What greater witness can you have than from God?
>
> And now, behold, you have received a witness; for if I have told you things which no man knoweth have you not received a witness?[1]

The Lord told him He knew Oliver's supplications and explained to Oliver the answer he had previously received from the Lord. By this, Oliver knew it was the Lord speaking to him through the Prophet, for only God and Oliver knew of the circumstance of which the Lord now spoke through the Prophet to Oliver.

I, too, had prayed to the Lord concerning my mission and the status of my parents. Only He and I knew of these, my supplications. I had not spoken of them to any other soul on Earth. In the patriarchal blessing, the Lord spoke to me, knowing what I had spoken to Him in prayer. He brought peace to my soul, He fully answered my prayers and confirmed to me that He knew me personally and was continuing to communicate with me. I knew then His will concerning me and I knew that He would continue to communicate His will to me.

From that evening on, my mind was firmly set that I would serve a mission as soon as I could after turning nineteen. I also had my mind firmly set—reset if you will—that I was going to try to serve and please the Lord the rest of my life. Since that time, I have tried to do so.

I remember once speaking to my niece, Kaye, shortly thereafter. After I responded to her question, she said, "Boy, Glen, you sure have become independent. When you decide what you are going to do, no one's going to stop you!"

I suppose she was right. When I have felt something was right, especially after receiving an answer from the Lord, I would become firm in pursuing that course of action. Hopefully, that has been the case all of my life since then.

I received a scholarship for more than full tuition, at the University of Utah. When I decided to serve a mission, I believed that I would lose that scholarship, for I would be leaving school after only one quarter. I went to meet with the Director of Scholarships to inform him that I would not be there for the next two years. He told me that if I did well during that first quarter and returned to college right after returning home from my mission, my scholarship would be saved and waiting for me! That was a wonderful surprise.

I also went to my boss. I gave him notice that I would be quitting work a few weeks before I left on my mission. He told me that he appreciated my dependability and the work I had done. He then said, "When you return, come and see me. If you want it, your job will be waiting for you. I am also the Director of a Department at the University, and I will let you choose to return to your current job or you may come and work for me on campus."

In the Book of St. Mark, Jesus instructed he who was to become His chief apostle, Peter. Peter spoke of the sacrifice he and the other disciples had made to follow the Savior.

> And Jesus answered and said, Verily I say unto you,
> There is no man that hath left house, or brethren, or
> sisters, or father, or mother, or wife, or children, or lands,
> for my sake, and the gospel's,
> But he shall receive an hundredfold now in this
> time, houses, and brethren, and sisters, and mothers,
> and children, and lands, with persecutions; and in the
> world to come eternal life.[2]

I felt this was true for me as well in what was happening. I had been willing to give up my job and scholarship, two years of my life and two years of progress at the university. But the Lord had returned it all to me and blessed me greatly in additional ways as well.

As I tried to honor the counsel of both my mortal father and my Heavenly Father, I went to one quarter of college at the University of Utah and then left on my two-year mission to France and Switzerland.

"Those exercises have only made your back problems worse."

The first nine weeks of my mission were spent at the Language Training Mission (L.T.M.), the predecessor of the current Missionary Training Center (M.T.C.) Back at the time of my mission, the first four weeks were normally spent learning the grammar of the foreign language. The remaining weeks were used to memorize discussions and scriptures for teaching people we would later meet on our mission.

My group finished the four weeks of grammar lessons in two and a half weeks. We then took the test that was given as a final for fifth-semester students at B. Y. U. Everyone in my group scored higher than the highest in the university class. This is modern-day evidence of the gift of tongues. After completing the remaining weeks of study, we flew to Europe. A number of us went to Geneva, the headquarters of my mission. Others went to either Paris or Brussels, the headquarters of their respective missions.

I was first assigned to serve in Toulouse, France, where I stayed for almost six months, and where I grew to love the French people. I was then transferred to Dijon, France, where my companions and I worked very hard, and had many wonderful teaching opportunities and saw a number of people gain testimonies and join the Church.

Our work consisted primarily of (1) Tracting—where we knocked on doors and explained Who we represented; (2) GQing—contacting men walking along the street, asking them the "Golden Question"—would they like to learn about our church? and (3) Teaching interested people the beliefs and principles of the gospel of Jesus Christ.

On a typical day, we arose at or before 6:00 a.m., showered, shaved, ate breakfast, studied individually and jointly, and left by 9:00 a.m. to go to the area of the city in which we would be tracting. If we had teaching appointments for the evening, we would return to our apartment by 9:30 or 10:00 p.m., and seek to be in bed by 10:30.

My third city was Marseille, France. While serving there, one day I went to the branch president's office at the chapel and lifted a heavy 16mm film projector from the back of a deep cabinet. I heard something pop in my lower back and a severe pain shot through my body.

That night, I rode home on my little motor bike in great pain. Every bump reverberated up my back and down my legs. The next day, I went to a French doctor, told him what had happened, and he immediately said, "I know what it is. I will give you a prescription for the muscle pain and show you exercises to do."

I took the pills for a while and faithfully did the exercises for the next several months. My back condition just worsened. I served several months in Marseille and then three more in Toulouse. I was then transferred to the mission home in Chambesy, a suburb just outside of Geneva, Switzerland. There, I went to a Swiss doctor, who said, "I think I know what it is, but let's take an x-ray to make sure."

The x-ray confirmed what he thought. When I showed him the exercises the French doctor had told me to do, the Swiss doctor said, "Those exercises have only made your back problems worse."

He demonstrated exercises that would have me stretch my back muscles in the opposite direction from what I had been doing for more than three months. He then prescribed twenty sessions of physical therapy. Over the next several months, I went to physical therapy twice per week and tried to exercise every morning as I had been instructed to do. It was hard, for during the next months I averaged only seven days per month at the mission home. The remaining days I was on the road, sometimes driving up to ten hours in a day. Obviously, sitting in a car for that long did not help my back. Neither did sleeping on hard floors in the apartments of other missionaries on those twenty-three nights per month while we traveled, holding zone conferences and presenting firesides in every branch in the mission.

I definitely do not intend to give the impression that my mission was only a trial. The fact is, my mission was one of the most wonderful and spiritual times of my life. I began it with a testimony of the truthfulness of the gospel I would be preaching to the people of France and Switzerland. That testimony only grew firmer and more unshakeable during that amazing two years of service to the Lord. As I taught and bore my testimony of this truth, the Spirit bore the same witness to the individuals I was teaching and to me. I saw miracles happen through the power of the priesthood I bear. My knowledge of the existence of God my Father, of His Divine Son, Jesus Christ, and of the truthfulness of His gospel grew ever stronger as I served.

I grew to deeply love the people I met—the French and Swiss, other missionaries and my mission president and his wife. To this day, many of these strong friendships still continue. Whenever I meet any of them, our strong friendships are immediately renewed.

At the end of my mission, I was determined to try to continue to be faithful and true to the Lord. I knew that through His atonement, the way was open for me to return to my Father in Heaven and have eternal happiness if I would obey the Lord's commandments.

I had my brothers schedule classes for me to begin only a few days after I returned from my mission. The Lord provided much for me as well. Shortly after my return, I scheduled and took a test that was offered for those who had lived for some time in a country whose language was not English. I passed that test and received twenty-five credit hours.

I also took additional tests for multiple, individual subject areas to test out of those individual courses. I passed all of the subject tests and received an additional forty-eight hours of credit! I came home from my mission as a second quarter freshman, and at the end of the first quarter after my mission, I was a second quarter junior! Thus, I served my two-year mission and I graduated from the university in only 21 additional months—a total of two years of college. So in a total of four years, I got both my four-year bachelor's degree and served a two-year, full-time mission. I feel that because of my desire to obey the desires of both my earthly father and my Heavenly Father, the Lord blessed me to accomplish both. It did take some hard work and good scheduling. I took very heavy loads—usually around 22 credit hours. I generally worked 25 to 35 hours per week at the same time. Moreover, nine months after my return home, I got married and served in multiple capacities in my church. I taught the sixteen- through eighteen-year-old Sunday school class, the Elders' Quorum, served as Y.M.M.I.A. (now Young Men) President and home taught seven non-member, part-member or less-active-member families.

I was very busy. But I was also very blessed. I was married to the person with whom I wanted to be for eternity. I had a wonderful and spiritually-rich mission experience. I was well on my way to completing the first phase of my college education.

CHAPTER FOUR

THE NEXT YEARS

Travel became a fun and educational
part of our family life.

After returning from my mission and continuing through the months after first getting married, Dianne and I talked about our hopes and desires for our future life together. We wanted to raise a large family, teach them correct principles, spend considerable time with them and give them great and diverse experiences. We mapped out certain things we would and would not do. Our first task at hand was to complete our bachelor's degrees. Then, my plan was to continue to receive my juris-doctorate in law school.

Among other things, I suggested that we try to travel widely and see as much of the world as we reasonably could. Dianne readily agreed with that suggestion. I told her that I did not want to buy a cabin or condominium for a vacation spot. Nor did I want to buy a house trailer or motor home. Instead, I would rather travel to all kinds of different locations, and stay in hotels or motels so we would not have to clean up after ourselves. I did not want to be bound to virtually always go one place, in order to justify paying the purchase price and thereafter, taxes, repairs, etc., of a cabin or condo. Nor did I want to only go somewhere close to home because we were towing a heavy trailer. This way, we would see many different places and cultures, because we would be free to choose. I determined to take Dianne on trips, go as a family on numerous trips and also take my children on additional trips to give them different cultural experiences and an education of the world. These trips would also serve to develop an extra closeness and legacy of experiences between us and each of our children. As our children grew, the plan included taking my oldest three children on long trips initially and the youngest three on short trips until they got a little older. Having taken Audrey, Becky and Craig to Washington, D. C. in 1989, I took Natalie, Anne and Emily thirty miles to Park City that same year. While I was away with one group, Dianne was playing and partying extra with the other group, and then vice versa. Travel became a fun and educational part of our family life.

Dianne and I went on numerous trips and we took our entire family on many additional trips. Through the years, we traveled to most of the 50 states and to more than 40 nations.

"We all have our own bedroom, but Mom and Dad have to share!"

In the 1985-1986 school year, there was a determined effort by the Jordan School District in which we lived, to change from the traditional nine-month school year to a year-round school schedule. During summers, Dianne and I tried to consistently work with our children most mornings and then play with them in the afternoons. Summer was also the time for us to take several trips together. So we wanted no part of year–round school.

I began looking for a home in another school district. I called the largest district in the valley and spoke with the deputy superintendent. He assured me that the very last schools in the district that could ever go year–round would be the two in the Holladay area. So I focused my searching in that area.

In the summer of 1987, I purchased a newer, larger home in Holladay, Utah. It had twice the number of bedrooms and baths than our home in South Jordan, some twelve miles away. My five-year-old daughter, Natalie, described to friends and neighbors our situation in this way: "We all have our own bedroom, but Mom and Dad have to share!"

After purchasing the home, I spent the next month with various contractors doing some remodeling. In the process, I lifted some 80-pound bags of concrete from a storage shed, across a lawn and into my pickup truck. Then at our new home, I unloaded and carried them around to the back of the home. That was a huge mistake.

Within less than two days, I could hardly walk. The back injury that commenced on my mission returned with a vengeance. A day later, I literally could not walk alone. The next day, right after Dianne left to take the kids somewhere, I carefully and painfully rolled out of bed, determined to see if the nerves going to my legs would allow me to stand, even if the pain was severe. With no one else at home, if I screamed with pain, no one would hear me. I put both hands on the bed to help me stand. As I boosted myself upward, using arms and legs in the process, I collapsed to the bed and floor after uttering an involuntary, but loud, scream.

Walking down even two steps into the garage to get into our mini-van, with Dianne under one arm and my oldest child, Audrey, under the other was so painful that I could not contain the scream that erupted from within me. Then, bending my head as I stepped into the van brought pain that was almost more than I could take. I went to a chiropractor, whose treatment helped—right after it hurt so much that I hoped to never need to experience it again.

For nearly two weeks, I either lay in bed with ice packs under my back, or I crawled to the bathroom or the kitchen. I ate my meals by kneeling on the floor with my elbows supporting the weight of my upper body while I ate the food off of a plate placed on the floor. Drinking required a straw, of course.

CHAPTER FIVE

COUNCIL BEYOND THE VEIL

"A council is being held right now to determine what to do about your request."

In order to spend time with Dianne and our children, I often brought work home in my briefcase. Except when I was serving in some church calling, I would spend the evening with my wife and children, and then, when everyone went to bed, I would open my briefcase, take files out, and work until midnight, one or two o'clock in the morning.

I intended to take my three oldest children to Europe in 1991. But in March 1990, I told Dianne I felt that I should take them the coming summer—in 1990—instead of waiting for another year.

To her question, "Why," I responded, "I'm not sure, but I just feel strongly that I should take them this year. So I made arrangements to do so. We left for Europe on Audrey's 16th birthday, July 23rd.

Then in May, Dianne awoke early one morning from a deep sleep, having the strong impression, "Glen is going to die and leave you all alone." After a couple of weeks, she told me, adding, "I felt the Lord had something for you to do on the other side of the veil."

I immediately began to fast and pray, and I went up to be alone in the mountains to plead with the Lord to allow me to live and to raise my children. I made promises to Him and received some very real and precious feelings and impressions through the Spirit. I wrote most of these down, and still hold them to be very special.

One of the impressions I received was that I would be allowed to live to raise my children. What a relief! Since I had lost both of my parents in just over three months' time while I was in high school, I did not want to have my children lose either of their parents. In fact, my mind would not even "compute" the thought of their not having a dad. What I did not realize was that my being allowed to live did not mean that I would not have serious, and even life-threatening problems not too much later. Nor did I know that I would come to wonder if those impressions were still in effect for me and my family, even less than a year after receiving them.

Six and a half months later, at the beginning of February 1991, and throughout that year, we learned well why it had been necessary for me to take my three oldest children to Europe the prior year. I had very serious health problems that would have prevented a trip to Europe that summer. I know that it was not eternally essential that I take these children to Europe. But I have come to know that the Lord grants us His tender mercies for both critically important, as well as, for eternally non-essential things. His love for us is so great that His mercy knows no bounds. If our faith and desires are right before Him, He will reveal marvelous things to us simply because He loves us, not only because those things are essential for our eternal well-being. Indeed, I have come to understand that, just as a loving parent on Earth does both important and less significant things for his child, simply because he loves that child, so do Father in Heaven and the Lord Jesus Christ bless us in both important and less significant matters.

What I learned in February was that I would suffer two heart attacks. On Wednesday, February 4, 1991, I was working in my office at home when I felt seized by a severe stinging, attention-grabbing sensation. It extended from my waist upward. I wanted to immediately get my hands and arms flat at my side and to have my entire body flat. The unpleasant feeling seemed to last nearly twenty minutes. Just as it was subsiding, the doorbell rang at the other side of my home. Our neighbor had come to borrow something. After I found it for her, I went back into my office, rested for a few minutes, and then resumed my work. That sensation did not return and I virtually forgot all about it—but only for a very short time.

I really just put the circumstance out of my mind and went on with things as though nothing had happened. In fact, the following evening I took my daughter, Becky, to a BYU basketball game. We ran from the car toward the Marriott Center. We stopped running only when Becky, not I, felt tired.

The following day, I did normal things. I took my vehicle to have some tires replaced. While the work was being done, I took my near-daily walk. When the walk was completed, the tire replacement was also done. I drove to the temple, where I served as a volunteer for nearly 30 years—with only a few leaves of absence for illnesses and hospitalizations.

That evening, I took Dianne to dinner and to a play with some friends. We got home kind of late, and it took me a while to fall asleep.

I awoke at 3:45 a.m. with an intense, tingling-to-stinging feeling from my waist up. Because of back problems, I slept on my back with several pillows under my knees. While sleeping on my back, I would generally have my hands up on my stomach. I immediately wanted to lie entirely flat—legs, arms and all. I did not even want to have my hands or arms up off of the bed. This time, the painful, tingling feeling was much more intense than it had been just sixty hours before. I awakened Dianne, who wanted me to go to the hospital. I didn't know for sure what was happening and resisted, until I began coughing up blood. At that moment, I decided to go to the hospital. I asked Dianne to call some relatives who lived nearby and ask them to meet us at the Cottonwood Hospital emergency room to give me a blessing. Then Dianne drove me there.

I stayed in the hospital for a week, until the following Saturday. During the time there, the cardiologist told me that blood work confirmed that I had definitely experienced a heart attack. I really felt badly that I was in the hospital on my daughter Anne's birthday, so I missed our traditional celebration. That is an important day for a six-year-old. That Friday, my last full day in the hospital, I had a stress test and angiogram that showed I had at least three very blocked coronary arteries and at least one-third of my heart damaged—gone.

On the prior Wednesday, Dan and Julia Skoubye (Sko-bee) came to the hospital while my brother, Jay, was there visiting me. Dan had been one of my counselors and then had replaced the man who succeeded me as Bishop. He was serving as our Bishop when we moved from South Jordan to Holladay. Dan asked, "Bishop, is there anything I can do for you?"

I responded, "Yes, you can give me a blessing. We have given so many blessings together and you know how I feel about them—I can ask for anything I want, as long as I am willing to accept whatever the Lord gives me. I want to live to raise my kids."

Jay anointed me, and Dan sealed the anointing and proceeded to begin the blessing.

The blessing began as most do. But before actually pronouncing any blessing, Dan paused for what seemed a long time. Finally, he said, "A council is being held right now to determine what to do about your request." He then spoke of my service in the church, my faithfulness to the Lord and about my request to live to raise my children being an unselfish one. It seemed that for quite a while he was just coming up with things to say, just biding his time. He was not blessing me—yet. He was just filling in the time, for I am sure he was waiting for further inspiration to find out what had been decided in the council. So was I!

He stopped talking again for quite a while, this time for longer than the first pause. Then he continued the blessing, saying, "I bless you to know that the determination has been made that your request shall be granted."

I could not hold back the tears. The Spirit there was so strong. And a wonderful blessing had been promised me. Dan would much later tell me that while he had his hands upon my head, he had the firm impression that "the Lord had something else He wanted me to be doing, but He changed His mind."

I believe the accurate way to consider this would be that although the Lord had something that I could be used in doing on the other side of the veil, because of His great kindness and grace, He would recognize and honor my faith, the faith of my family and of those giving me the blessing. I had asked, and it would be given to me, according to my faith.

President Wilford Woodruff confirmed the existence of councils being held in heaven—or the spirit world—for the purpose of determining who should be taken for assignments on the other side of the veil. One of the considerations in these councils is how much one is currently doing on Earth and whether it would be more important to leave a person in his current and/or future earthly responsibilities than to take him at this time. Another consideration would undoubtedly be the faith of the individual and of others who are praying—on this, and even on the other side of the veil—that he may be "spared" and left on Earth. President Woodruff stated:

> I have felt of late as if our brethren on the other
> side of the vail had held a council and that they had said
> to this one, and that one, "Cease thy work on earth, come

hence, we need help," and they have called this man and that man. It has appeared so to me in seeing the many men who have been called from our midst lately. Perhaps I may be permitted to relate a circumstance with which I am acquainted in relation to Bishop Roskelley, of Smithfield, Cache County. On one occasion he was suddenly taken very sick, near to death's door. While he lay in this condition, President Peter Maughan, who was dead, came to him and said: "Brother Roskelley, we held a council on the other side of the vail. I have had a great deal to do, and I have the privilege of coming here to appoint one man to come and help. I have had three names given to me in council, and you are one of them. I want to inquire into your circumstances." The Bishop told him what he had to do, and they conversed together as one man would converse with another. President Maughan then said to him: "I think I will not call you. I think you are wanted here more than perhaps one of the others." Bishop Roskelley did not go to him. By and by this [second] man recovered, and on meeting Brother Roskelley he said: "Brother Maughan came to me the other night and told me he was sent to call one man from the ward," and he named the two men as had been done to Brother Roskelley. A few days afterwards the third man was taken sick and died. Now, I name this to show a principle. They have work on the other side of the vail; and they want men, and they call them. Now, my brethren and sisters, those of us who are left here, have a great work to do. We have been raised up of the Lord to take this kingdom and bear it off. This is our duty; but if we neglect our duty and set our hearts upon the things of this world, we will be sorry for it. We ought to understand the responsibility that rests upon us. We should gird up our loins and put on the whole armor of God. . . .[3]

"Yes, I will take over [his] responsibilities . . ."

While I was in the hospital, my former, original first counselor, Scott, died and his funeral was held while I was in the hospital. I could not even attend his funeral.

Several years after I received this blessing, Scott's widow called me to give her a blessing. Since I was going to be near her home the next morning, I told her I would be happy to stop at her home prior to going to my commitment at the Jordan River Temple.

Lois' sister answered the door and showed me to the bedroom where Lois lay. I greeted her and we talked for a while. I asked about her specific needs and then asked if I could use another room to pray and prepare myself to give her the priesthood blessing she had requested.

In two places in The Book of Mormon, the Lord explains what a priesthood bearer should do to prepare himself to perform any priesthood ordinance. This would certainly apply to the priesthood ordinance of administering to the sick or otherwise afflicted. He instructs:

> The words of Christ, which he spake unto his disciples, the twelve whom he had chosen, as he laid his hands upon them—
>
> . . ., saying: Ye shall call on the Father in my name, in mighty prayer; and after ye have done this ye shall have

power that to him upon whom ye shall lay your hands, ye
shall give the Holy Ghost; and in my name shall ye give it,
for thus do mine apostles.[4]

This instruction was for His disciples, who held His
priesthood, for preparing themselves to receive power to perform the
ordinance of giving or blessing an individual with the Gift of the
Holy Ghost. The same directions would certainly apply to one's
preparing himself to bestow any—all other blessings—through the
authority of the holy priesthood.

In the next chapter of The Book of Moroni, the Lord
instructs elders in His church as to how they should prepare
themselves to ordain others to the priesthood:

> After they [the elders of the church] had prayed
> unto the Father in the name of Christ, they laid their
> hands upon them, [those who were to be ordained to
> a priesthood office] and said: . . .[5]

Just as in the prior citation of two verses, the same counsel is
given by the Lord to priesthood bearers for preparing themselves to
perform an ordinance through the holy priesthood.

Thus, I knelt in mighty prayer in order to prepare myself to
give Lois a blessing by virtue of the priesthood I bear.

In my prayer, I sought three specific things. Nothing else was
on my mind. The only matters on my mind were:

(1) I sought to have the Holy Ghost with me that I might
speak with power from God through the priesthood authority I held;

(2) I asked for the inspiration and direction of the Spirit to
direct me to say that which the Lord desired I say in blessing his
daughter, Lois; and

(3) I prayed that I might be authorized to bless her with
specific blessings, including improved health and vitality, that she
might be made better through that priesthood administration.

31

As I prayed, I received a firm impression from the Spirit. During the council being held during the blessing I received in the hospital from Dan Skoubye and my brother, Jay—the council to determine what to do about my request—a council member called upon my counselor, Scott, who had just entered the spirit world, and asked him if he would take a specific assignment for a time. The impression I received of Scott's response to the issuance of that assignment came in these words:

> Yes, I will take over the responsibilities that Bishop
> Park would be given if he were taken from the Earth. When
> he does come, I will step down, and he can take over.

That response was certainly what I would expect of Scott. He had no agenda but to serve the Lord however He wanted him to serve. He was not worried about the title or position he was given. Whether the position was big or small—in others' minds—Scott was perfectly willing to serve where and how he was asked to serve.

"I did not want to die without a current recommend."

Prior to leaving the hospital, and at my first appointment with the cardiologist after returning home, I was told that I should have bypass surgery after waiting for six to eight weeks. That length of delay would allow my heart to recuperate and strengthen some before having another serious hit to my heart.

While in the hospital, my Bishopric came to visit. At the end of their visit, I asked the Bishop if he could interview me for a temple recommend. Mine would expire later that month and I did not want to die without a current recommend. He complied.

"You look like you're dead!"

A doctor in my stake advised me to get a second opinion from a different cardiologist. He recommended Dr. Robert E. Fowles, a cardiologist at the Salt Lake Clinic, who worked with most of the general authorities of my church and visiting foreign dignitaries who have heart problems. After I met with Dr. Fowles, he arranged for me to have a thallium stress test done on March 28, 1991. The stress test part of it, walking on a treadmill, was very easy for me. Then, they injected thallium into my bloodstream and had me lie on my back on a table with my arms raised above my head. A technician took pictures of my heart and its blood flow from the left side with a type of x-ray camera. Within seconds of raising my arms, I told the technician that this was not going to work. He said that he had to finish getting the images and that it would only take about ten minutes or so. Within minutes, I suffered flash pulmonary edema—

sudden lung distress—and was rushed by ambulance to the L.D.S. Hospital. The pulmonary edema triggered a serious heart attack.

The doctors at the hospital were unable to stop the heart attack that had begun that morning during the thallium stress test. When they gave me something in my I.V. to try to stop the heart attack, my blood pressure immediately plummeted, and I nearly died. The cardiologist and surgeon there made it very clear that I had to have coronary bypass surgery immediately. The associate surgeon told Dianne, "It is either a trip to the operating room, or a trip to the mortuary!"

So I waited, still experiencing severe chest pain, until nearly 8:00 p.m., when the heart surgeon had finished the other surgeries he already had scheduled that day. Then, they prepared me for mine. As I was being pushed on my hospital bed to the operating room, I passed my brother, John, and my dear wife, Dianne. I tried to be positive and to smile as I passed them. I still remember the encouraging words my brother said. I remember the loving things Dianne said and the expression of concern on her face. I wondered if I would live to see her again.

In the hall, immediately outside of the O.R., the anesthesiologist asked me how I was feeling. I told him, "Fine, except it still hurts here," pointing to my chest, near the bottom of my heart.

He replied, "In just a matter of seconds you won't feel it anymore." He injected something into my I.V., and within seconds, I was out.

When I awoke, I was in the Coronary Intensive Care Unit. I had a huge tube in my mouth that went down my throat. I was so groggy and felt completely weak and sick everywhere. It took a number of seconds before I remembered where I was and what had happened. I had undergone quadruple-bypass surgery. The large tube going into my mouth and down my throat seemed to be making me choke. My first impulse was to fight it in my attempts to breathe. But within moments, I remembered something my brother, John, had told me following his own bypass surgery. He had told me of his having that same impulse and of his own efforts to fight it until he was told that the tube was helping him to breathe, not keeping him from doing so. So I quit fighting the tube and let it do its job. Even though it was helping me breathe, it was very uncomfortable and annoying, and I continued having the impulse to fight the tube.

The next several days were extremely difficult. I could not raise myself from lying down without the strong assistance of one or two other people. If I attempted to use my own back and abdominal muscles to sit up, they would pull on my sternum—which had been cut open—and its muscles, some of which had also been cut. The pain was excruciating! So whenever I needed to move, sit up or get out of bed, one or two people had to slip their arms behind my back and lift me. They insisted that I not try at all to even help lift myself. After the first time trying to help just a little, I understood why. Any attempt on my part brought immediate, unbelievable pain. Every part of my chest hurt, in spite of the strong pain medication I was receiving.

I had complications in breathing and had to have a respiratory technician come and work on me during the night. It was extremely painful to have someone pounding on my back in an effort to open up my lungs with my sternum having just been sawed open.

It was so nice to see my family come to visit me on Sunday, about 36 hours after the surgery. But I just cried when I saw them, and I saw the horror and anguish in their eyes when they saw the gray color of my skin and tubes going into my nostrils. I really didn't know then how very horrible I actually looked. But a few days later, I was moved to the Coronary Care Unit. I was allowed, after being helped out of bed, to walk into the bathroom alone. The nurse still waited outside in my room. I looked into the mirror and was really startled at what I saw. I said aloud, "You look like you're dead!" It was so very depressing to see how dead I really looked.

While in the C. C. U. several days following the surgery, I started vomiting and then dry heaving. The pain in my chest from those repeated convulsions was incredible. It weakened me so much. I really felt miserable. I wondered if I was going to live.

Every time I went down to the rehabilitation room, I got depressed. There I was—a 40-year-old—on oxygen and doing worse than the 70- and 80-year-olds who had undergone the same surgery. But I was as I was, and I couldn't change that. These other men had had the same surgery, but they had not suffered a massive heart attack the very same day as their surgeries. My doctor said, "Having that double hit to your heart was more than many hearts can take." It had definitely damaged and weakened mine, and the rest of me as well.

In 1991, the little monitors that clip onto a finger to measure the level of oxygen in the blood were not as accurate as they have come to be. Therefore, in order to know that they had very accurate results from testing the level of oxygen in my blood, a doctor would push a thick needle down into an artery that was approximately a quarter inch below the skin between my wrist bone and the next bone on my hand that is located at the very top of my thumb. He had to push and probe for what seemed like forever to get to the artery, and then he would draw out some blood. Because my blood oxygen was low, this very painful procedure was repeated several times. The probing and pushing were done in the same place each of the times following the first. That spot grew ever more tender, for the area was bruised and extremely sore each time before he would even begin the probing.

I had to stay in the hospital some extra days, for I was not getting enough oxygen to my body because of the weakened state of my heart. Even when I was allowed to go home, I was on oxygen for a month. When I walked into our house, I felt great emotion, for I was so happy to be back home.

I returned home on a Saturday and seemed to improve for the next several weeks. I started walking in the house, tethered to a long oxygen tube. At first, I walked for only a few minutes each day. After the month on oxygen, I still walked inside for a while, because it was cold outside. Plus, whenever I walked down only to the end of our driveway, I had to walk uphill in order to return. Even that slight slope made it extremely difficult for me in my weakened condition.

During the weeks following my bypass surgery, during which time my heart was supposed to be able to recuperate and strengthen some, I walked through my house as my doctor had recommended. One day as I was walking, I stepped on a rug next to the side door of my house. I did not see a straight pin sticking up in the rug. Because of the weight of my body, the pin sank deep into my heel. It really hurt. I leaned against the wall, for my balance was not good, and I did not dare twist my body or to try to sit down on the floor. Because my sternum had not fully fused, such twisting would have caused immense pain. And I would not have been able to stand back up by myself from sitting on the floor. I brought my foot up so I could see and reach the pin. I pulled and pulled to get it out, but I was so weak and the pin was so far into my foot, that I struggled to get it out. I pulled and pulled. I summoned every ounce of energy I could, and I tugged again. The pin came out, and I sunk to the floor, exhausted and hurting.

After a short rest, I had to have help to be able to stand. I limped to a sink and washed the wound in my foot. I walked so as to not let that part of my foot touch the floor until I got a bandage to put on it. I continued into my bedroom, walking the same careful way, pulled a pair of socks from a drawer, and put them on. I wanted to keep the wound clean in order to prevent infection. I certainly did not need that in addition to everything else!

"I am far more concerned about your living for the next three months than I am about your living for the next fifteen years!"

Increasing the time I walked each week, I finally pushed it up to 45 minutes each day. I was getting more and more encouraged. I was becoming stronger and experiencing less and less pain. Then, in the first week of June 1991, the week that my daughter, Audrey, went to Cedar City for Girls' State, I went into heart failure. Dianne and I had intended to drive four hours to go to the graduation ceremonies and then bring her back home with us at the end of the week. But now, experiencing heart failure, I could not go, and Dianne didn't feel that she could leave me. So Dianne's parents went to the ceremony. Immediately upon seeing them, Audrey asked, "What's wrong with my dad?" I don't know if their attempts to reassure her were totally effective. Later that same month, I again suffered a more severe occurrence of heart failure, but obviously, I lived. While it was occurring, however, I wasn't certain that I would live through it.

During that time, my cardiologist went out of town for a seminar. I came to understand that my condition was very serious, maybe even precarious, for he called me every day, sometimes more than once in a day, to see how I was doing and to determine whether I needed an additional prescription or anything else.

Shortly thereafter, during one of my appointments with Dr. Fowles, he reviewed the normal things a cardiologist asks a patient whose condition is anything but normal. I then asked him questions about diet and things I should and should not be eating. At each of our previous appointments, I had asked similar questions and had suggested various foods, etc. This time, my doctor answered my dietary inquiries in this way: "You already know more about diet than most of the cardiologists practicing in the country. You are weak enough that I think you should eat anything that looks or sounds good to you. I am far more concerned about your living for the next three months than I am about your living for the next fifteen years!"

I understood his message. I needed to focus on living and growing stronger. Worrying about a heart-healthy diet could wait until I was strong enough to live through the next several months.

During the months following my first heart attacks, every day I lived with the prospect of dying at any time. I was very weak and unable to do much. For some time following my bypass surgery, I would get out of bed, eat breakfast, and then return to my room to rest. After that rest, I would shower and shave. Then I would rest again. Following every activity, however simple and easy for a healthy person, I needed to rest. I was not a healthy person.

For six-to-eight weeks following my surgery, I was not to bathe in a bathtub. I had multiple long incisions—where my chest had been cut open, incisions in my left leg, from which the veins had been harvested for three of the four bypasses and an incision above my heart to remove the mammary artery. Plus, holes had been cut for placing drain tubes in the lower part of my chest cavity. Therefore, because I was so weak, for the first three months, I put a stool in the shower so I could sit while I showered. Even then, I was very fatigued by the time I finished.

Because I was so weak and so limited in what I could do, it was easy to become discouraged, even depressed. I am certain Satan tried his very best to take advantage of my weakness and this potential for discouragement.

But my nature is not to allow myself to be emotionally down for long. I spent as much time as possible in activities with my wife and children. I made certain that I had things to which I could look forward. When I had a hard time falling asleep at night, or when I awoke during the night and had difficulty falling back asleep, I would think of what I wanted to eat for breakfast. After eating breakfast, resting, showering and shaving, I would think of what small snack I would have prior to lunch. While taking my morning walk, I would think of what I would have for lunch. Shortly after that, I would plan what I was going to do with Dianne or our children. Then, I would think about my afternoon snack, then dinner, what movie Dianne and I would watch and then my evening snack. In addition, when my children had any game, I went to watch them play. Although it may sound like I ate a lot, the fact is that my meals and snacks were very small. I could not eat a great deal at one time. So to keep up my strength and to try to gain back some of the weight I had lost, I needed to eat small amounts multiple times each day.

It should be obvious that I enjoy eating. In addition to looking forward to eating, I came up with other things I could look forward to doing. I am convinced that having things to anticipate helps one to keep a positive attitude and to avoid discouragement. But there is another, even more important element to my avoiding discouragement. I prayed with faith and trust in the Lord. I expected—trusted—that He would answer my prayers through the Holy Ghost and that I would receive the Spirit's comforting influence. Although my life did not just become easy, and my problems did not just go away, I did receive the comfort and buoying up for which I prayed. With that comfort, I continued to also pray for the Lord's blessing of health. Then I waited on the Lord for His answers and help.

In chapter 3 of the Book of Daniel, the account is told of Nebuchadnezzar, King of Babylon, causing a large golden image to be made. He commanded that at the sound of various musical instruments, all people, nations and languages were to fall down and worship that golden image. Anyone found not doing so would that same hour be cast into a burning fiery furnace. When the sounds issued, three captive Jews: Shadrach, Meshach and Abed-nego, did not fall down, nor did they worship that false god.

The king's advisors told him of the actions of those three young men. The king "in his rage and fury commanded to bring" them before him. He asked them if the charge was true. He continued, telling them if they would:

fall down and worship the image which I have made;
well; but if ye worship not, ye shall be cast the same hour
into the midst of a burning fiery furnace; *and who is that*
God that shall deliver you out of my hands?[6]
(Emphasis added.)

Their response is significant and impressive.

Shadrach, Meshach, and Abed-nego,
answered and said to the king:

O Nebuchadnezzar, we are not careful to
answer thee in this matter. *If it be so, our God*
whom we serve is able to deliver us from the
burning fiery furnace, and he will deliver us out
of thine hand, O king. "But if not, be it known
unto thee, O king, that we will not serve thy
gods, nor worship the golden image which thou
hast set up.[7] (Emphasis added.)

These three valiant and faithful men had determined that they
would only worship the Lord. They knew the Lord had the power to
save them. But even if the Lord did not save them from the wicked
decree and the imminent, painful death threatened, they would
remain faithful and true to the Lord their God. Their "But if not,"
represented the feelings I determined I would have as my own.

I hope I could say I felt the same feelings expressed by these
three faithful followers of the only true God. I was determined that I
would fight to remain faithful and not murmur or complain against
the Lord for not keeping these difficult times from coming to me. I
was also determined to not allow Lucifer to win in his evil and jealous
desires to lead me down to his despicable level.

CHAPTER SIX

PREPARING THINGS IN CASE I DIE

"Even without your law practice,
this is a full-time job!"

Prior to my heart attacks, I had gone through years of pretty continuous progress in building my law practice and my other self-managed investments. After my heart attacks and bypass surgery, and even more so after going into heart failure, I lived every day without a certain answer to the question, "How soon will I die?"

I went through the process of liquidating and consolidating my holdings. I met with someone to ask him if he would help

Dianne with my investments and financial affairs if I were to not live through these health problems. I reviewed with him what I had to manage in addition to my law practice.

He looked overwhelmed, and said, "This is a full-time job, even without your law practice!"

He was right. So I immediately began to reduce the number of things that needed active managing. It was not something that could be done in a day, in a week or even in several months. But I started the process. The process added one more thing on my list of things I needed to do each day. While I was working to sell and consolidate, each matter still needed its usual managing.

There was another element to my wondering if I would live for very long. I had received a priesthood blessing that promised that I would live to raise my children. But it really looked as though I may not do so.

I prayed and prayed with every fiber of my being that I might live and be healthy in order to share life with my dear wife and sweet children. I reviewed over and over in my mind the blessing Dan had given me. Although I sincerely believed it was inspired by the Lord through the Holy Ghost, it did not appear to be happening. So, in addition to continuing to pray with great fervor, I turned inward to examine myself. What if the Lord had intended it when he authorized and inspired the blessing but had determined that the promise would not continue because I was not worthy of it? Unworthiness has always been a basis for the Lord withdrawing His promised blessings. Was this the situation with me and the promise I had been given?

I could hardly bear my emotional pain. I was unable to handle the thought that I might not obtain the promise of being able to live to raise my children because I was unworthy. If my children had to grow up without a father because of my unworthiness, I truly felt that I would be miserable forever. I would never forgive myself for the suffering I would cause them and Dianne.

Therefore, I repeatedly expressed to my Father in Heaven that I had examined myself. I felt that I had gone through the process of repentance for everything I could come up with for which I might need to repent. I asked for His forgiveness, over and over again.

I prayed, "Dear Father, if there is anything more for which I need to repent, please tell me. Let me know what it is, and I will repent of it. Please." This was not my prayer on only one occasion. It was the subject of my conversations with God multiple times every day for many weeks.

I waited every day for His answer, telling me what I should do, the thing or things for which I still needed to repent. No feeling or impression came. Since I was not getting better, I remained uncertain whether an answer was forthcoming that would instruct me of what more I needed to do, or whether the Lord was simply going to bless me in His—not my—time frame.

"But after your children are raised, I wouldn't give a plug nickel for your life!"

On one of the first Sundays of July, I got up and started getting ready to go to church. After showering, shaving and eating breakfast, I began dressing for church. All of a sudden, I started feeling really sick. I told Dianne I would not be able to go to church. I then got back into bed. When Dianne and our children left for church, I rolled out of bed and onto my knees. I prayed for a long,

long time. I pleaded with my Father in Heaven that I might get better and be able to live to raise my children. I must have been praying for more than an hour.

At length, I received an answer—a firm impression that I would now begin to get better and stronger. I felt so much better that I wanted to show the Lord my appreciation for that definite answer. I got dressed and went to church. As I entered the hallway and walked into the foyer, I had a feeling that the Bishop would want to talk with me. That didn't bother me. I just thought "Oh." I entered the chapel just before Sacrament Meeting was to begin. That meant I had been home praying for almost the entire length of the first two parts of the block schedule of church—for more than an hour and a half.

After Sacrament Meeting, my Bishop came down the aisle, and greeted me. He asked me if he could come to my home later to visit with me. I said that would be just fine, keeping my smile to myself about having already known that he would ask this. Later, he came to my home and sat down with me. He told me that he, the bishopric and ward council had been praying for me for months and had never felt much of an impression about my health improving. But this morning, when they prayed, they felt, for the first time, that I was going to start getting better. Now, my Bishop had told me of receiving the same answer I had received, confirming what the Lord had told me earlier that day, while I was praying. While my Bishop was still speaking with me, the phone rang. Bishop Dan Skoubye was on the phone. It was he who had come to the hospital in February and who had blessed me that I would live to raise my children. When Dianne answered his call, he told her, "I awoke this morning with Bishop Park on my mind and I haven't been able to get him out of my mind ever since." He asked if he could visit me that evening. Dianne asked me if I felt up to having another visit—from Bishop Skoubye and his family. I told her, "Yes, of course."

When he and his family arrived, he told me the same thing he had said to Dianne. Then he said, "I feel every bit as certain as when

I had my hands on your head at the hospital that you are going to get better and live to raise your children."

There was my third witness of the same answer in one day!

In 2 Corinthians, the Lord says, in pertinent part: "... In the mouth of two or three witnesses shall every word be established."[8]

What a wonderful and kind blessing from the Lord. From that time on, I did start doing better and better, growing ever stronger. It was not an overnight process, but I did improve, with even my heart's ejection fraction increasing from about 25 up to 40, approximately eighteen months later. (A healthy man's ejection fraction is between 55 and 70. An ejection fraction of 25, according to one nurse, means that one's heart is basically non-functional. I continued to have problems from my "nearly-non-functional heart," but I did generally keep getting better and stronger. What a great blessing from a wonderful God.

In addition to the confirming witness that I would now get better, Bishop Skoubye added, "But after your children are raised, I wouldn't give a plug nickel for your life!" Obviously, that statement was not a comforting one to me.

> ... there were four or five times
> ... when I should have died.

School started that fall for my children. My oldest daughter, Audrey, was a junior in high school. Becky and Craig were at the junior high. Natalie was in elementary school. Anne and Emily had not yet started kindergarten. I drove to pick up Audrey many days after school and I picked up Becky and Craig from junior high school. I looked horrible. I was still very weak, pale and skinny. I did not look much better than when I told myself I looked as though I was dead. I must have been an embarrassment to these young children. To make things worse, I was driving a seven-year-old car. So I decided to do something about that part of the picture.

I could do only very little about how I looked. I needed to get healthier, but I was already doing all I could about that. I followed my doctor's directions. I ate carefully and exercised. I prayed. Beyond that, the biggest part of my improving was not really up to me. I could at least pick my kids up in something that looked decent. So, for a number of reasons, I bought a new and nicer car. In addition to wanting to look more presentable, I decided I would declare to the world and especially to my wife, my kids and myself that I was going to be around for a long time to enjoy driving it. I may not have looked very good sitting behind the wheel, driving it. But maybe people, especially young people, would look more at the car than at me. If they did, it would not be so potentially embarrassing for my children to be getting into the car with me.

When I told my children my reasons for purchasing the car, they liked my declaration that I was going to live for a long time. But they all told me they were not embarrassed to be seen with me.

It took approximately eighteen months before I had "passed the bubble," as my cardiologist called it. I was exercising and taking certain medications, but otherwise, I was supposed to be taking it easy. As I wrote above, my heart's ejection fraction finally rose to 40, and it looked like I would continue to get better and stronger. An ejection fraction of 40 was still a long way from 65 or 70, but it was far better than 25. At 40, my heart was at least functional, if not strong. It was not until that time—some eighteen months after my bypass surgery—that my cardiologist told me there had been four or five times during that time when I should have died. Although he had done everything that the best medical studies and tests could indicate was necessary for my condition, there was no real medical reason why I had not died.

I knew the reason was that my family, friends and I had prayed with faith. I had received a priesthood blessing, given under the inspiration of the Spirit and with the consent and authorization of the Lord. And the Lord had kept His promise given in that blessing.

"For example, I would not suggest that you go to Brighton and hike up to a lake."

During an appointment in September 1991, my cardiologist instructed me about what I should and should not do. Among other things, he said, "I want you to continue to walk daily on level or flat surfaces. Do not walk on steep inclines. For example, I would not suggest that you go to Brighton and hike up to a lake."

I immediately interrupted, "Do you know what I did last weekend?"

"No," he answered. "What did you do?"

"I went to Brighton and hiked up to a lake." It may sound contrived, but he literally warned against doing exactly what I had just done the weekend before.

"Really? he responded, looking deeply concerned.

"In fact," I said, "I had one of my daughters on my back."

"Really? How did that go?" He was obviously concerned.

"Fine."

"I would not suggest that you ever do that again," he advised. The expression on his face showed he was very serious.

"I have a question," I said. "Why could I do that when I have lost so much of my heart?"

"In my opinion, you started with an iron-man heart. If it were not for your clogged arteries and the damage done by the M.I.'s—myocardial infarctions—your heart would be fine and very strong. You were able to do that because, despite having lost so much of your heart and the rest of it being weakened, it is still stronger than most others would be after having gone through as much as yours has."

For the most part, although I had continuing problems, I slowly continued to get better and stronger during the next months. But still, I was not doing great. The tests I continued to have, including echo-cardiograms showed very little improvement. As I already said, finally, about eighteen months after the start of this horrible period of time, my ejection fraction had finally reached forty. I had finally cleared "the bubble." Dr. Fowles now felt I had a decent chance to live for some additional years. But in his mind, it was still a chance—not a certainty.

CHAPTER SEVEN

I NEED
A NEW HEART!

I did, indeed, need a new mitral valve, but that would not solve my problem. From what he could tell from reviewing my file, I actually needed a new heart!

I continued to live, getting stronger, little-by-little, for the next eight years. Audrey, Becky and Craig graduated from high school. Audrey and Becky graduated from college. Natalie was in high school and Anne and Emily were in junior high school.

In 1997, Audrey married David Dutcher. We welcomed David to our family. It was not easy to have my first daughter leave home for good.

Then things abruptly changed sometime in November 1999, while my son, Craig, was on his mission in France. I remember feeling something once or twice during that month that hurt quite a bit in my chest, but the pain quickly passed, so I simply paused and went on with the physical work I was doing.

On the first Saturday of December 1999, Dianne and I hosted the Park brothers' Christmas party. We prepared all day for the party, including cleaning the house, loading and carrying upstairs eight large tables and fifty metal folding chairs. Then, following the party, we returned the tables and chairs to my church. I returned home and helped Dianne clean up the upstairs and bring food, serving dishes, pots and pans downstairs to the kitchen. Then we put food away. Dianne washed dishes and I dried. I felt almost as though I was going to die. I was totally exhausted and felt pain in my chest and sick to my stomach.

The following week, on December 8th, I had a routine appointment with my new cardiologist, Dr. Douglas Ridges. When he listened to my heart, he said that he heard something very different from before and wanted to schedule an echo-cardiogram. I had that performed later in December. I really started feeling miserable all over again. While I ate my breakfast cereal, I would pause before finishing and rest my head down on my arms on the table. I felt so tired—exhausted, really. I started having real problems sleeping. I had to be propped up in bed in order to be able to breathe very well, or to sleep at all.

When I called Dr. Ridges and described my symptoms to him, he asked where I lived and told me he would bring me some medication on his way home from his office that day! I told him I could come in to get it. He asked if I had a cell phone and then gave me his cell phone number so I could call him when I arrived at the hospital office wing in which his office was located. He told me he would immediately come out to give me the medicine. That was very nice of him. His insistence on doing that and the tone and urgency in his voice made me realize that he felt my condition was extremely serious, even life-threatening. It was difficult for me to actually believe that I could be in such a serious condition. But I was.

The medicine helped some, but in reality, my condition continued to deteriorate. I got so I could hardly get enough oxygen. If I even said a full sentence, I would generally be out of breath. That was even when I was speaking normally and breathing as normally as I could. Dr. Ridges met with me and told me that his review of the echo-cardiogram indicated that I needed to have the mitral valve in my heart replaced. He wanted me to meet with Dr. Kent Jones, the heart surgeon at the St. Mark's Hospital. When I met with Dr. Jones, he told me he had looked at my file, including the echo-cardiogram. I did, indeed, need a new mitral valve, but that would not solve my problem. From what he could tell from reviewing my file, I actually needed a new heart! He would not dare operate to replace the valve, for my heart would not be able to withstand the rigors of the surgery and still recover. He ordered an angiogram and heart catheterization to be done on Friday, the 4th of February 2000. I had to take life very carefully for the next weeks.

My daughter, Audrey, was with her husband, David, living in a suburb of Boston. David was attending Harvard Law School. He was in his fourth semester—his second year—there. On the night before my scheduled procedures, I called her and told her I would be having those procedures done the following morning. She was really rattled. I tried to be reassuring and confident, but she could read between the lines. She knew that I had not been feeling very well for more than two months. Having these procedures only made everything sound worse.

When I told my daughter, Becky, who worked at the Utah Valley Regional Medical Center, she asked, "What is going on? I see people go in for these things, and some of them don't come out alive." I tried to reassure her. I don't think it worked very well.

That same night, I also told Natalie, Anne and Emily, who were still in high school and junior high school. I assured them that there was no big problem with what I would undergo the following morning. I did not want them to go through what one of my children had in the 8th grade when I was hospitalized following my second heart attack in February 1991. After the fact, I had learned from the history teacher at a parent-teacher conference that he had not understood why my child, who was such a good and consistent student, had failed a test in his class. When I checked the date of the test, I saw it was during that week when I was in the hospital after suffering my second heart attack. He said, "If I had only known, I wouldn't have made her even take the test. He was considerate enough to drop that score from her record and grade her based upon her performance on all of the other tests and assignments.

I did not yet tell my son, Craig, who was living in France, serving as a missionary. By the time he would get the follow-up letter, telling him the results of the tests, he would have suffered through more than a week of worry and wondering.

The doctor, wanting to sound unalarmed, told me that my blood pressure had dropped some.

The next day, I went in for the two procedures. While I was in the operating room having them done, the cardiologist performing the angiogram and heart catheterization asked if the incision in my upper leg hurt any. I said, "A little." So he had a nurse put some valium into my I.V. Immediately, I started to feel very sick. I saw the doctor order the nurse and technician to hurry and get this and that, and to do several things. They stopped the flow of valium, and added something else to the I.V. The nurse gave the doctor a syringe, which he put into the I.V. in my groin and rapidly and repeatedly tapped the I.V. connection. The technician inserted something into the second I.V. in my left arm. The doctor continued to hurriedly tap on the attachment at the end of the I.V. and catheter for some time. He also continued to nearly shout orders to the nurse and technician, who were both executing his orders as fast as they possibly could. I found myself praying silently and then watching what was going on as much as I could from my position on the operating table.

After several minutes, things seemed to calm down. The nurse went back to doing her routine tasks in the room, instead of being right next to the doctor or responding to the orders he barked out to her. The technician, who had come to be right next to my left arm, moved away and also started doing his normal duties. The doctor ceased frantically tapping on my lower I.V. and catheter. Only then did I casually ask what had happened. The doctor, wanting to sound unalarmed, told me that my blood pressure had dropped some. I asked, "How low?" He replied, "Oh, to around 50." I do not know to which side of 50 it dropped. But I do know that with blood pressure around 50 over something, two things happen: one soon loses consciousness, and if things do not quickly improve, he dies! Although the whole event had been scary, I had lived through it.

When the doctor came to see me in the recovery area following the procedures, he told Dianne and me in no uncertain terms that I needed a new heart. Nothing else would resolve my condition. He was frank and unequivocal. There was no doubt that the only thing that would resolve my serious and deteriorating health problems was to receive a heart transplant. I waited in the recovery room for the necessary recovery time to pass, and Dianne took me home. During the procedures, at my request, Dianne had gone home. Audrey had called her to say that Harvard Law School had a program that would allow a student, in the case of a family medical emergency, to complete the final year of law school at another approved law school and still graduate from Harvard. But it would require immediate action that would need to be completed within a week's time. The following Friday, all of the paperwork would have to be submitted or there could be no chance for approval. He would need to make written application, and my doctor would need to write a letter, explaining the nature and seriousness of my condition. Plus, David would need to be accepted by the other approved law school. All of those things had to be completed in seven days!

I asked Dr. Ridges if he would write such a letter. Because of the time crunch and with his consent, I prepared and delivered a proposed letter to him, telling him that if he wanted to do so, he certainly could discard it, or modify it in any way he chose. He quickly returned his letter for me to review and send off to Harvard. He had indeed changed it. What he wrote explained that things were much worse than I had written! I had thought the condition I had described was dire. His explanation portrayed it to be considerably worse.

Harvard approved David's transfer to Brigham Young University College of Law so that he and Audrey could be close to me since I could die at any time. But that was only the first step. BYU told David there was a slim chance they would accept anyone more to become part of their senior class and that it would take several weeks to reach a decision. David and Audrey needed to know sooner than that, for they had to inform Harvard of BYU's decision, plus renew their apartment lease for an additional year or let it expire.

Because of this need to know, when I learned of Harvard's decision, I called the Chairman of the BYU Law School Admissions Committee and told him of the circumstances. I explained David's qualifications and of the urgency of the situation. When initially applying for admission to law school, David had applied to both Harvard and BYU. David had been accepted to BYU with those who were at the same point David was in law school. So I reasoned with the committee chairman that David was obviously qualified. He was very courteous but said that he only had one vote on the committee. He assured me that he would speak with all of the other committee members and would try to reach a determination in as few days as possible. I thanked him and said, "Good-bye."

That afternoon on the same day, David received a telephone call from the BYU Admissions Committee, telling him he had been accepted to attend the BYU College of Law for his final year!

"You might need it tonight!"

The angiogram and heart catheterization were done on Friday, February 4th. That weekend, my family fasted and prayed for me. On February 19th, Dianne and I met with Dr. Dale Renlund, the Director of the Heart Transplant Program at both the L.D.S. Hospital and the University of Utah Medical Center. During our hour and a half meeting, he explained much about the program. While we met, my insurance company told their financial assistant that such a transplant would be covered, but only at the University of Utah Hospital. An appointment was set up for me to meet with one of the cardiologists there and to begin receiving medication in an effort to help stabilize my condition. At the end of our consultation, Dr. Renlund wrote a telephone number on the back of his business card and handed it to me. He said this was the number to reach the hospital and to be able to ask for the nurse coordinator of the heart transplant program on call twenty-four hours a day. I asked when I might need that. He responded, "You might need it tonight." That certainly grabbed my attention!

After that meeting with Dr. Renlund, I had to do a terribly difficult thing. My son, Craig, was nearly at the end of his mission in France. Our plan had always been that Dianne and I would go to pick him up and tour some with him before returning home. My unhappy task was to inform Craig as delicately and as optimistically as possible that we would not be able to do so—and why. I wrote the letter and carefully made several revisions so it was exactly as I wanted it. After writing that I would need a heart transplant, I wrote that perhaps I would get the heart of a 17-year old. "Then, after not very long, I'll once again be able to take you on the tennis court!"

I mailed the letter, and multiple times each day I prayed that when Craig received my letter, the Spirit would buoy him up and give him peace. Craig and I have always been very close. I knew that this information would scare and worry him. Since it took six to eight days for a letter to go one way, he would not know how I was doing for at least another week. Anything could happen, and he may not hear anything reassuring for so very long.

Just before the time when Craig would receive my letter, I called his mission president and explained to him my situation, told him of the letter I had sent to Craig and told him that I knew the letter would "knock Craig down" when he read it.

President Wilcox replied, "Elder Park is a strong young man. He knows why he is here, and he will hold up just fine."

I agreed with President Wilcox's assessment of Craig, but asked if he would tell the missionaries at the mission office to transfer to him any call they might receive from Craig, wherever he was, and if he would accept any call Craig might make after he read my letter. He assured me he would do so.

I thanked President Wilcox, and then continued to pray for peace to be given Craig.

It took more than two weeks for me to receive Craig's response to my letter. He wrote, "Today, I received letters from two of the people I love. One was from [one of his sisters] and the other was from Dad. Reading Dad's letter was really hard. But I then went into my bedroom to pray for Dad. During my prayer, a feeling of great peace came over me."

I was so relieved and grateful. I went into my room and prayed sincerely to express that gratitude to my Father in Heaven for answering my prayers in Craig's behalf.

Craig continued to pray and to be concerned for me. I continued to pray for him and to keep him up to date—in as optimistic a way as I possibly could.

Before mid-March, when I had my first clinic appointment with the Transplant Department at the University of Utah Hospital, I improved quite a bit. I was certain that my improvement was due to the faithful fasting and prayers of my immediate and extended family. The doctors there started me on a regularly-increasing regimen of Coreg, a relatively new and extremely strong medicine given to serious heart failure patients. I immediately experienced severe side effects from the medication.

Each time I took the Coreg, my sinuses felt as though they were tightly over-stuffed with gauze or something—almost to bursting—and definitely beyond just hurting. My whole head hurt. I felt nauseous and overwhelmingly fatigued. I found that I should simply plan to take a nap immediately after taking a dose, for I became not only totally fatigued, but I ached all over—especially in my head. I had absolutely no energy. My head and even my eyes really hurt. I needed to sleep between 45 and 120 minutes—especially at first.

I started on a twice-daily dose of 3.125 milligrams. After two weeks, my body was starting to adjust to the Coreg. Then, my dosage was doubled, to 6.25 mg twice per day. My body had to start adjusting all over again. My body's reaction to the higher dosage was the same as when I first began the initial dose. The increases in dosages continued every two weeks—next to 12.5 mg twice daily, then to 18.0 mg, and finally to 25.0 mg twice each day. With each increase in dosage, I experienced the same renewal of the severe side effects, which would begin to subside near the end of two weeks on each respective dose increase. So, for ten weeks time, I had serious and continuing side effects. I felt great fatigue and sickness the entire time.

With the combination of a priesthood blessing, my prayers and those of my family, the best medical care available and the blessings of the Lord, I began to grow stronger and to have greater energy.

In May 2000, Craig returned home from his mission. It was such a joy to see him and to have him home again. Though I was still experiencing the effects of the continually-increasing dosages, I was doing well enough to spend time with him and the rest of my family.

In June 2000, I again felt the need and the opportunity to declare to my family and myself—even the world—that I intended to live. I did this in a number of ways, including the purchase of another vehicle. My family was excited. They all seemed to really like the idea. It may seem silly, but my family literally seemed lifted by my purchase and declaration.

CHAPTER EIGHT

THE PROCESS OF DYING

I continued to vomit and then dry heave day and night for months.

My slow, sometimes-halting, improvement continued for nearly four years. In November 2003, I scheduled flights and a trip to Myrtle Beach, South Carolina for Dianne and me. Our plan was to leave January 6, 2004. In December 2003, I told Dianne I had an impression that we should not go. She asked why. My response was simply that I really felt we shouldn't, and when I rely on such feelings, I never regret it. Dianne had many years before come to accept my having such impressions and the decisions I made in reliance upon them. So I cancelled our reservations.

I was hospitalized for the first of many times in 2004 on January 10th. If Dianne and I had gone to Myrtle Beach, we would have been there, perhaps stranded and with me requiring hospitalization in South Carolina—far away from the Heart Transplant Department of the University of Utah Medical Center and my home and family.

It was determined that I was in atrial fibrillation. One of the functions of the atria—the two upper chambers of the heart—is to help regulate heart rate. When the heart is damaged and becomes weakened, it usually expands in size. The heart is the only muscle in the body that grows weaker, not stronger, as it gets considerably larger. As the atria get bigger—and weaker—they lose muscle tone, and in various situations, under a variety of circumstances, may cease to have distinct or strong contractions. Instead of contracting in a proper rhythm (sinus rhythm) the atria may contract irregularly or merely flutter. Fluttering atria are in fact racing, but accomplishing very little. This atrial fibrillation is usually not life-threatening in itself, but in an end-stage heart failure patient, it can cause much more serious problems—even death. I learned that my condition was not just the atria contracting extra fast. Because the walls of the atria were so weakened, they were simply fluttering extremely rapidly. As such, they were not performing their function of moving blood to the ventricles.

For the ventricles to receive adequate blood flow, the atria must push the blood into them through valves within the heart. My fluttering atria were obviously not doing the job, and my condition continued to deteriorate.

From Saturday, January 10th, through the following Monday morning, my doctors tried in several ways to correct the atrial fibrillation, without success. On Monday, the 12th of January 2004, they performed a procedure called cardio-version. This involves a doctor holding electrical paddles on rubber pads previously placed on the chest. The heart is then shocked with electrical current to force it back into normal sinus rhythm.

This procedure is not always successful, and even when it is, atrial fibrillation sometimes returns after only a short period of time.

In my situation, the procedure worked, and my heart returned to sinus rhythm.

But only that one problem was resolved—and only temporarily. Everything else wrong in my health remained as it was. And things were, very soon, to get much, much worse.

A typical action taken for a heart failure patient following cardio-version to reverse atrial fibrillation is to follow up with a medication that tends to help maintain sinus rhythm. I was given one of the most common, amiodarone. I soon learned it is a very toxic medication. What followed were not the desired results. This medicine, coupled with my serious and deteriorating condition, caused me to start nearly three months of vomiting. I vomited day and night. And when I had nothing left to vomit—which was most of the time—I would proceed to dry heave, sometimes continuing to do so for minutes at a time. I continued to vomit and then dry heave day and night for months. Amiodarone must not have been the sole reason for my vomiting and heaving, for I ceased receiving it only days after my cardio-version. But the vomiting and dry heaving continued for three months. With my heart basically non-functional due to its overwhelming weakness and limited capacity, none of my organs were functioning well, for none of them were receiving adequate blood flow. There was only one week during the entire first half of the year when I felt somewhat better. But then, just as quickly as that week had begun, it ended. Again, I began to feel poorly, and then I got even worse, and then considerably worse.

Because of my rapidly worsening condition, my doctors, consulting with other specialists, determined to implant in my chest a bi-ventricular defibrillator. This would be implanted by first making an incision above my heart, just inside my left shoulder. The surgeon would then form a "pocket" within the several layers of epidermis— the outer layers of the skin forming one side of the pocket—and the inner layers serving as the pocket's other side. The bi-ventricular defibrillator would then be dropped into that newly-created pocket above my heart and the top sutured closed. In addition to serving as a pacemaker, it also had two wires that ran to my ventricles—the lower two chambers of my heart. These wires would allow the defibrillator to shock my heart should it either stop or go into irregular contractions.

January 26th was the first day I was scheduled to have the implantation performed. Dianne took me to the hospital on that Monday morning and I had the necessary preliminary preparations done, including the placement of an I.V. in my arm and a blood draw. The blood draw was to determine if my blood was "thick" enough. The higher the blood's international normalized ratio (INR) level, the thinner the blood is. The surgeon would implant the device only if the level of my blood's "thickness" was 1.9 or lower. He would have preferred that it be 1.5. My blood's INR level was over 2.0, so the surgeon refused to perform the implantation. The I.V. was removed, and I returned home, to take certain medicine and to eat certain foods to try to get my blood thicker.

The process of doing this was to be assisted by having me not take any type of long-lasting blood-thinning medicine. Instead, because I did need to have something to keep me from having blood clots that would surely bring on a heart attack and kill me, I was to have Lovenox injected in the abdomen twice each day. Its blood-thinning effect lasts only 12 hours. The shot was very painful. In my weakened and extremely thin condition, the pain was greater than normally might be the case. It stung a great deal. That stinging would continue for at least 45 minutes after the shot was given. The area around the spot—not just the spot where the shot was given—remained tender and very sore for weeks thereafter. The area turned black and blue and remained so for weeks. I dreaded receiving these shots each morning and evening. But, I remained alive, and my blood thickened to below 1.9, so the next time I went in to have the defibrillator implanted, the doctor proceeded with, and completed, the procedure.

Now I had a metal device the size of a small cell phone placed in a man-made pocket in my chest, inside my left shoulder, and approximately two inches below my collar bone. Obviously, the area of the incision and implant was very sore for a period of time. But instead of becoming less sore, it became continually more so. I withstood the increasing pain, and waited for the appointment set for me to go in to have the implanted bi-ventricular defibrillator examined by the doctor who performed the implantation.

When I went to the follow-up appointment at the implant surgeon's office, he was out of town. The instant his nurse looked at the spot, she knew there was a problem. The area was infected. She obtained a prescription for a strong antibiotic to treat it.

Dianne took me to the hospital two days later, and the implant surgeon examined the site. The medication was not cutting the infection, so I was hospitalized for three days and put on a stronger antibiotic, administered by I. V. At the end of those three days, I had a pique line inserted into my arm and threaded to my heart. I was then released to go home, and Dianne had to attach a spherical ball full of antibiotic to the I.V. end of the line each morning and evening for the next ten days. Each time the round container was attached to the line, I had to keep it elevated for the next hour in order to get all of the medicine to empty into my body.

If this did not work, then the defibrillator would need to be removed, the area cleaned, and a new defibrillator would be implanted. Then the hope was that there would be no continuing or additional infection.

The infection apparently was mostly cleared up, but the site of the incision needed further work by a plastic surgeon to cut out the upper part, clean, disinfect, and re-do the closure. Apparently the reconstructive surgery was successful, but the entire area was even more painful and required several additional weeks to heal. There was a second time, to be described next, when I needed to go through the same period of having those horrible twice-daily shots in my abdomen.

I was so weak and already in pain, but each shot would further deplete my energy and require some time of rest. By this time, it did not take much to further reduce my strength and vitality or increase my pain.

The months of January, February and March were an extremely difficult period for me. For the most part, I vomited and dry heaved day and night. I could hardly keep down anything I ate. During this time, my health declined quickly and continuously. In March, I had an angiogram done, which normally takes between 45 and 60 minutes to complete. During the procedure, it was found that I did have a seriously blocked coronary artery. In the hope of having that blockage corrected, which would assist my heart in performing better, the cardiologist determined to place a stent in the artery. Because the coronary arteries were deteriorating and clogging, the blockage was in a spot to which it was very difficult to get the stent in place. The doctor struggled unsuccessfully in his repeated attempts to place it. It hurt within my chest each time he tried to get the stent through the artery and into place.

I silently prayed so hard and so many times. Ultimately, I ended up being in the cath lab—or operating room—for nearly three hours. When the doctor said he would try just one more time, my prayer became all the more urgent. The stent finally went into place. We would have to wait for only a short time before we would see whether this procedure would make any difference in my condition. I did know that the procedure had totally worn me out. I was so fatigued. It took me several days just to recover from the toll it took on my body and heart. Unfortunately, it did not seem to cause any real improvement in my condition. My heart and overall health continued to deteriorate.

One secondary purpose in placing the stent was to be able to check off the last procedure that might be done to help my failing heart short of a heart transplant. Therefore, in exhausting this last-ditch treatment effort, I was in a position where my doctors and the transplant staff could begin having me undergo the tests necessary to determine my qualifications to be placed on the heart transplant list.

The tests involved many different things to show definitively that my heart was doing so badly that it really did need to be replaced. The rest of my organs and body had to be functioning sufficiently well—aside from their needing additional oxygen-filled blood from the heart—to warrant getting a second heart. Obviously, a good second heart would not be wasted on a body with one or more other organs insufficiently strong to do their part to sustain that body's life—whether there was sufficient blood flow or not. The tests were often strenuous and hard to endure—at least to one in my condition. I generally experienced pain. I always ended up fatigued—more fatigued than I already was.

My body was retaining fluid, for my heart was incapable of pumping it out of the body. In a very short time, my stomach and organs were virtually swimming—drowning—in retained liquid. I was, in reality, drowning in my own fluids! Because my organs were immersed in fluid, as well as not receiving adequate oxygen or nutrition, they continued to function less and less well.

Even my taste buds were adversely affected. Any water I drank had to be extremely cold. If I drank any without several ice cubes in the cup, I felt that I might throw it right back up. I very soon could hardly stand to eat most of the things I had always enjoyed eating. For example, Dianne baked me my favorite chocolate cake on Valentine's Day. After only one bite, I knew I could eat no more of it. That was a first for me. Neither could I stand to eat many other foods. I had always liked Mexican food, but now it was repulsive—even sickening—to me.

Though I could not stand to eat most of the things I had always enjoyed, I craved almost anything with raspberries in it—raspberry jam, raspberry swirl cake, raspberry juice, sherbet, ice cream—whatever.

Soon though, I had a hard time eating at all. Nothing tasted good. In fact, any food I ate tasted bad. It did not stay down. For example, many times I struggled to eat a very small quantity of mashed potatoes with butter. I had to virtually force down every bite. Because I was restricted in how much I could drink, my mouth was always dry. That made it all the harder to swallow relatively dry mashed potatoes. After pushing myself, for I really needed to get some nutrition, I would sometimes be able to finish most of the extremely small serving of potatoes. Shortly thereafter, I would vomit it up and then dry heave for a while.

Sometimes, when I dry heaved for a lengthy period, I would pass out. Several times, my heart would even stop. Fortunately, the Lord allowed, or caused, my heart to restart, and I—although in the process of dying—would continue to live a while longer.

Entering the third day of this hospitalization, I reached fifty in my count of needle insertions.

During this period from January through June, my oldest daughter, Audrey, was in the beginning months of the pregnancy of her second child. She was nauseous most of the time, and while visiting us, would go to a bathroom and vomit. She came to visit from Washington State many times, each time thinking that it may be the last time she might ever see me alive.

Several times, Dianne would hear someone vomiting and run to the bathroom from which the sounds were coming to make sure I did not lose consciousness and die. Sometimes, when she would get there, she would find Audrey, not me. Sometimes, she would find me and would stay there until I finished vomiting and dry heaving in case I passed out or my heart stopped.

I was hospitalized seven times in the first half of 2004. Although there were brief times of improvement, generally, my health continued in a precipitous downward spiral. Indeed, the process of dying proceeded with virtually no interruption. During one of my hospitalizations, I made it a point to count the number of times one type of needle or another was stuck into one of my hands or arms. Entering the third day of this hospitalization, I reached fifty in my count of needle insertions. I stopped counting, although the needle sticking certainly did not stop.

Usually during a hospital stay, it was necessary to have the I.V. changed every two or three days. With a combination of factors: my heart hardly working, my entire cardiovascular system in poor condition, my blood pressure so low and my veins beginning to collapse, one such change of I.V. required seven different attempts, with three different nurses trying to get it in and functioning. One such complicated I.V. replacement ended with it requiring a doctor to finally get it inserted. Another concluded with a male technician, known in the cardiac care area to be the "resident expert" in placing intravenous needles in long-term patients, finally getting it in place. Of course, the weaker, thinner and sicker one is, the greater the pain he or she feels when any needle is stuck into the body, especially the I.V. needles, which are larger in diameter than the needles used to either give the patient a shot or draw his blood.

Furthermore, the thicker needle is pushed a certain distance into the vein, not just down to the vein. Often times, the I. V. needle would hit a valve in the vein. This brought additional pain and meant that the nurse would need to pull the needle out, stop the bleeding and try again somewhere else.

Following several months of hospitalizations and a steep decline in my health and my heart's strength and viability, I had lost over forty pounds. I weighed quite a bit less than I had in high school—and I had been very thin in high school.

CHAPTER NINE

WARM-BLOODED

"I'm okay. I'm used to being
in this type of temperature."

All my life, I have always been the last in a room to feel cold. In fact, I am generally too warm when everyone else is comfortable or even cool due to the temperature. The following experience will illustrate. During the winter of 1980-81, while I was serving as Bishop in my ward, I met at 6:00 or 6:30 every Sunday morning with my two counselors, executive secretary and ward clerks. Many Bishops' offices in our church buildings had their own separate heater/air conditioner that was generally situated behind the Bishop's desk. This allowed a Bishop to be in his office working or meeting with his members or counselors during the week, without having to heat or cool the entire building to a fully comfortable level.

During one such early-morning, wintertime meeting, one of my counselors—Dan Skoubye, in fact—was seated several feet from me, dressed in a suit coat and tie. He said, "Bishop, could I interrupt for a minute?"

"Certainly," I answered.

"Would you mind if we turned the heater on? I'm freezing."

"Of course I wouldn't mind. I'm sorry you feel cold. I feel just fine. In fact, I'm even perspiring some. Is anyone else cold?"

I looked to my right, at my other counselor, Brent, who was a meat cutter. Each day, he worked in a cool-to-cold room next to a freezer where the meat he worked on would be hung and stored.

He smiled and said, "I'm okay. I'm used to being in this type of temperature."

Further embarrassed, I proceeded to an assistant ward clerk. He responded, "I've started wearing thermal underwear to these meetings, so I'm okay."

My ward clerk declared, "I get kind of cold. But I go home after these meetings and sit in front of the fireplace."

I felt so badly. "I'm so sorry," I said. "If anyone ever gets cold, interrupt me or anyone else who is talking and either have me turn on the heater, or come and turn it on yourself. I never had any idea this was happening to you men."

I would continue to fight to live and to seek His divine help to be able to do so.

With that background about my body temperature, let's return to 2004. Being so thin, and with my heart pumping insufficient warm, oxygen-filled blood to my body, I was almost always cold, especially my hands and feet. Sometimes, I would shiver uncontrollably. I frequently asked to be covered as I sat in my recliner. Dianne or my child would tuck the blanket right around my neck and legs to cover every bit of my body below my head. Since I could not breathe in a flat position, I could not lie in my bed. Even wrapped in one or more blankets, it would generally take quite some time before I could become comfortably warm. Even then, my hands, arms, feet and legs would generally remain cool, and they always hurt. Dianne would periodically rub or massage them. This brought temporary, semi-relief. But the pain never fully left and would very soon return to its full intensity.

Though I was praying so hard—pleading with the Lord and asking that He would help me—it certainly appeared that my life was about to end. The Lord had many times blessed me to get better and continue to live. I felt the Lord had blessed me over and over for so many years. But the time may have come, or was soon to be, when those blessings would end. Therefore, sometime in February, I approached Father in Heaven in fervent, pleading prayer. I told Him that I wanted to live as much as I ever had. Although my children were no longer as young as they had been thirteen years earlier, they still needed me and the help and support I could give to them. I realized that many other needy children in so many other families lose their father or mother, or both. I knew that sometimes those children were at least as young as mine had been when I had received the priesthood blessing in 1991. I also knew that the Lord loved those children and their parents. But I was still pleading with Him that I might continue to be blessed to live.

I sincerely asked that I might get better. I told God that although I wanted so badly to be with and support my wife and children, I knew He had blessed me so very much to allow—no, to help me to live—and that I appreciated it greatly. Now, I still wanted to live. But if it was His will that I should die, I would accept that. I would accept His will, and I would not complain or murmur at all or in any way. I explained that, notwithstanding my willingness to accept His will, unless He told me unquestionably so I knew for sure that it was His will that I die, I was going to fight to live. If He wanted me not to fight to live, all He would need to do was to tell me—not with some incredible sign—but in the same way He had communicated with me on so many occasions throughout my life. And if He told me, I would quit fighting, and again, I would not complain or murmur, but I would praise Him and His name forever. But until I got such an answer from Him, I would continue to fight to live and to seek His divine help to be able to do so.

"We will never be alone so long as we know how to pray."

For some time, Dianne had been deeply worried as she saw me get sicker and weaker, suffering extreme pain as my body continued to go through the process of dying. She did not want to lose me, but she could hardly stand seeing me suffer so. Each morning, she went to an empty bedroom upstairs to read the scriptures, the *Ensign* magazine and to pray. The fear that had dominated her thinking since 1990 was that I would die—and leave her alone. The thought of being alone scared her—haunted her.

One morning in March 2004, while in prayer, she heard a male voice call out "Dianne." Believing it was me, she responded, "What?" But there was no answer. So she arose from her knees, went to the door, and opened it, only to find no one there. She hurried downstairs to our bedroom at the other end of the house. She found me more soundly asleep than I generally ever was. Assuming that it must have been the only other male in the house, our son, Craig, she went upstairs to his bedroom and found that he was also asleep. She returned to the original bedroom and continued to pray, wondering whose voice she had so distinctly heard.

Over the next weeks, Dianne continued to wonder, and she prayed to know whose voice she had heard. Then one morning while reading the *Ensign*, she read a talk that had been given by Elder Joseph Wirthlin, of the Quorum of the Twelve Apostles. Nearing the end of the talk, Dianne received the answer she had been seeking. Elder Wirthlin quoted from the Book of Revelation: "Behold, I stand at the door, and knock: if any man hear my voice, and open the door, I will come in to him, and will sup with him, and he with me."[9]

Elder Wirthlin continued with the declaration, "We will never be alone so long as we know how to pray."[10]

Dianne's eyes filled with tears as the Spirit confirmed to her that this was the answer to her weeks of prayerful questioning and of her years of fearing I would die and leave her alone. If Dianne continued to have a personal relationship with the Lord, she would never be alone, for the Savior would sup with her and she with Him!

This marvelous experience gave Dianne the strength and ability to finally tell God that, although she wanted so badly for me to live and to be with her, she could hardly stand to see me suffer so badly. Therefore, she told Him that she would turn her will over to the Lord. If it was His will that I die, she would—now could—accept it. She would accept His will over her own.

"There must be something we can do!"

Apparently, my other organs passed all of the tests they needed to, and my heart failed all of the tests necessary for me to qualify for a heart transplant. In other words, if I received a second heart, my other organs would continue to work. It would be a waste of a good heart to have the patient die soon thereafter from some other organ failure. Yet, my heart had to be in bad enough condition that it would not get better. As I said, I passed and failed everything necessary to qualify to be put on the heart transplant list.

On April 6, 2004, I was told by the coordinators in the Heart Transplant Department that I had qualified under federal regulations for a heart transplant. A representative of my insurance company, Altius Health Plans, had on a number of occasions visited me in the hospital. She told me, my wife and one or more members of the hospital transplant unit that when the necessary paperwork was sent to Altius, everything would be ready to move forward and my heart transplant would be covered. All that would be needed was for the hospital to submit the pre-authorization paper work. Within only several days of when the paperwork was submitted to Altius, both the transplant unit and I received a telephone call from someone at Altius with a devastating response. Altius, instead of giving such pre-authorization, stated that such a procedure would NOT be covered. Nor would it cover any of the follow-up treatments, procedures or medications required after such a non-covered procedure.

There would not be any insurance money to cover a transplant. Federal regulations require that if a person's name is put on the transplant list, when that person is next to receive a transplant, he or she must receive it, whether or not there is money to pay for it. So my name was not put on the heart transplant list. My hospital wanted to make sure there would be money available to pay for any transplant they would do. After all the painful tests and all the assurances from Altius, I would not be able to receive a transplant!

I felt then and I still feel that Altius Health Plans lied to us, and further did everything necessary to shirk their responsibility to pay for what had been a covered procedure. They used a permitted method to comply with Utah law to get out of this responsibility that was rightfully theirs. But their "legal manipulation for technical compliance" did absolutely nothing to satisfy their moral or ethical obligation. I would never recommend them to anyone. But I was stuck with them. With my medical history, no other insurer would agree to insure me.

My brother, John, later told me that when he informed his son, my nephew, Bret, of my situation, Bret responded, "There must be something we can do!

In fact, there was not much that could be done.

My condition continued to deteriorate more rapidly all the time. There appeared to be little chance that I would live to receive the only thing that would extend my life—a heart transplant.

"Dad, you do not fight to make it through this day, you fight to make it through this moment, don't you?"

My son, Craig, had begun working for me in April 2002, after he received his Bachelor of Arts degree from the Marriott School of Management at Brigham Young University. During these months of my decline, I reviewed with him the things he would need to know to help his mother and also to continue as much of my work as possible in the event of my death. I showed him where things were, wrote out in much detail how to do what would be needed following my death. I gave him many instructions. One was to contact my clients whose original estate plans I had and inform them of my death and that they could come to pick up their original documents and be given the names of attorneys I would recommend to assist them in my place.

I prepared a list of things that needed to be finished or coordinated with certain clients on pending matters. I listed all of my business and financial accounts and wrote directions of what to do with each of them. My lists included directions for short- and long-term projects.

Since my son, Craig, had worked for me for the two years since he received his bachelor's degree, he was with me every day when I was at home. Often times, when he would come into my bedroom to go over business matters, he could only stay for a few minutes, for it was apparent that I had run out of energy and even the ability to focus on such matters. Craig would need to leave me to rest. He would proceed to take care of the business affairs in which we were involved, without my further involvement at that time.

One day, Craig, having observed my deteriorating health, and having watched me fight for months to continue to live and breathe, said, "Dad, you do not fight to make it through this day, you fight to make it through this moment, don't you?"

My answer was very simple: "That's right."

"When you can't breathe, nothing else matters."

During the first months of 2004, because my heart was in near-complete failure, I had great difficulty breathing. This was especially the case at night. At first, each night when I lay down on my bed, it often took only seconds until I could not breathe. So I had pillows placed under my back and head, to prop me up. Otherwise, I could not breathe. This is a very frightening experience. When one cannot get breath, it feels as if he is drowning or being choked without hands, but choking nonetheless. I will repeat that thought—this is an extremely frightening experience.

During these months, I referred clients to other attorneys, one after another. By the time this year would be over, I would have lost most of my clientele. During the first several months of 2004, I sat as much as possible during the day. I could hardly breathe when I lay down. Because of all the sitting, my weakened back hurt all of the time. When I would do the reduced amount of work I was still able to do, I would often move my chair out of the way, place two pillows on the floor in front of my computer desk and kneel to type. If I sat more, my weak and sore back muscles would spasm. Sometimes, I could not kneel for very long. Some days, I could not work at all. Other days, I pushed myself to do as much as I could—probably more than I should. It did not take very long each day before I was so fatigued, that I could do no more. Sometimes, "not very long" amounted to only minutes.

Soon, I would need to sit in a recliner in my bedroom anytime I tried to sleep. If I would recline very far back, I would cease being able to breathe. In time, it became necessary for me to sit up straight with my back totally vertical in order to get sufficient breath. Initially, on many nights—and then nearly every night—it was necessary for me to stand up during the night in order to breathe. Of course, it was impossible for me to sleep while standing up. Plus, after standing for so long, I would start feeling that I was going to pass out. I remember distinctly looking at a clock in the room when I stood up, and then again, when it felt that I could breathe adequately. This often took nearly an hour! Again, I cannot adequately express how very scary it is when you cannot get enough air! Suffocating really grabs your attention! As a radio advertisement states, "When you cannot breathe, nothing else matters."

Obviously, when one cannot breathe, he does not sleep well. During these months, I averaged barely two hours sleep each night. That amount of sleep time was not all in one block. It was obtained by adding multiple short blocks of time that were interrupted by lying awake for longer periods of time throughout the entire night. Indeed, nights quickly came to be a literal nightmare. Even though in the evenings I became so tired, I dreaded going to bed. I knew that I would have to fight all night to sleep and even to breathe.

Every night I dreaded the time when bedtime approached— every night—for I knew that I would go through yet another horrible and horribly lonely, frightening and death-threatening night. Every succeeding night brought exactly the same lonely, frightening, long and threatening experiences. I cannot really describe how much I prayed, how urgent and pleading my prayers were, or how dependent I knew I was on the Lord. When I could not breathe, I would sit up to get sufficient oxygen and would pray fervently for the Lord's help. I knew without any doubt that only He could help me. Only He could save me, not just ultimately—eternally—but during all of the numerous "moments" through which I was fighting to live.

If I cut or bumped myself, I would likely bleed to death, internally or externally, before anything could be done.

My doctor, and those who worked with him in the heart transplant unit, tried many different treatments—probably all of the things they could come up with—just to keep me alive. My doctor prescribed a dozen different medications, one after another, in his attempts to resolve a whole slate of health issues that continued to arise and threaten my life.

I had frequent blood draws to test all kinds of levels in my blood. Regularly, the draws were used to determine such things as: levels of sodium, potassium, chloride, CO_2, creatinine, glucose, calcium, magnesium, iron, anion gap, blood urea nitrogen (BUN), tacrolimus, international normalized ratio (INR) (coagulation—thickness/thinness) of the blood; white and red blood cell levels; levels of numerous medications in my blood; levels of cholesterol and other lipids; and other important components in my blood.

At one draw to determine the levels of numerous substances in my blood, the phlebotomist drew sixteen or seventeen tubes or vials. Afterward, I only half-jokingly stated, "I can't remember whether she drew sixteen vials or two quarts of my blood!"

I was given several different medicines to "thin" my blood. The blood's "thinness" or "thickness"—its INR—is discovered by analysis after a blood draw.

Because of the blood-thinning (anti-coagulation) medications I was taking, I was told the desired level for me to have any surgical procedure was 1.5. As previously written, the higher the INR number, the thinner the blood. On at least two occasions, my blood INR measured at or near 9.0! At each of those times, I was told that I must be extremely careful. If I cut or bumped myself, I would likely bleed to death, internally or externally, before anything could be done. Since I was vomiting and dry heaving so much—followed by passing out—it was very possible that I could pass out, bump my head and die without anyone even knowing until hours later. Dianne and Craig told me that when I needed to go anywhere, I should get them to help me, even during the night. I should awaken one of them, and they would help me. It was hard for me to awaken them during the night just to help me to walk into my bathroom.

> ... I feel that when I see Him there,
> it will only confirm what I now know—
> that He lives and is my Savior."

After one appointment with my cardiologist, Dr. E. Michael Gilbert, I was sitting outside the exam room. The Transplant Department social worker sat down with me and talked for a while. In our conversation, she asked me, "How do you continue to get through this?"

I answered, "Because I have a deep and abiding faith in Jesus Christ."

She quickly responded, "I'm not a religious person."

I said, "I understand," and said nothing more. I wanted her to be able to say whatever she wanted to say, whatever it was her job to say to me. I was not going to preach to her. Her response appeared to close the door to further discussion of my beliefs. I was going to respect her desire to not hear any more about them.

Then, she asked me additional questions about my beliefs, and I answered them truthfully and as succinctly as I could. Although I was very careful to not be pushy about my beliefs, I answered her truthfully, unafraid to speak freely of my faith in the Lord Jesus Christ.

My answers included, "I know that I am a son of God. I know that Jesus Christ is my Savior. Every day, I pray for comfort, and I actually receive comfort from the Spirit that buoys me up and gives me the strength to keep fighting and to maintain hope. I have already experienced miracles in being preserved thus far. My faith is that either the Lord will continue to preserve me, but if not, He will give me strength to make it through the final process of dying. And then, I know that I will someday stand before Him to be judged. I know He loves me. And honestly, I feel that when I see Him there, it will only confirm what I now know—that He lives and is my Savior."

This dear woman said something to the effect of, "I see."

She said nothing negative about what I had said. Our discussion ended as I went on to the next thing I needed to do at the hospital that day.

All over again, I would be totally under the control of this invisible, retching power.

During these first months of 2004, and indeed for the prior thirteen years, the Lord had repeatedly allowed things to get about as bad as they could, and then He would step in and preserve my life.

This happened, over and over again. I experienced many miraculous interventions that saved and preserved me.

During a time when my INR was at 9.0—six times thinner than the desirable level, one night I awoke and could tell that I needed to vomit. Not wanting to awaken Dianne or Craig, I walked quietly around the bed and went into the bathroom, alone. I closed the bathroom door so Dianne could sleep, and I vomited over and over again. This bathroom that only I used was very small. Other than the whirlpool bath and toilet, there was insufficient space for me to lie down flat in any direction.

I continued to vomit. When I could not vomit anymore, I proceeded to dry heave for a period of time. I could not control the convulsions. I could not stop heaving. Every time a convulsion would start, it felt like my stomach was being both smashed and also pulled up into my chest by some unseen, malicious hand, intent on pulling it through my throat. I hardly finished one huge convulsion before the next would begin all over again. Each one caused my entire body to tighten up. When one ended, I would think I could relax. But almost before the thought could be considered, the next convulsion would grab me and my insides. All over again, I would be totally under the control of this invisible, retching power. Every convulsion would sap energy from my already-depleted body. Because I did not start with much in the first place, before long, I had absolutely no energy left. I continued to convulse until I passed out.

I awoke some time later, lying on the floor, my knees raised and my head right in the very corner of the room, where the bathroom door casing was on one side and the linen closet door casing was on the other side of a 90-degree angle. My head was so close that I could feel the hair on my head touching the door casing of the door on each side of my head. Somehow, although I had passed out and fallen back, my head had not hit either casing. Had it done so, I almost certainly would have bled to death, or had such a huge hematoma inside my skull as to damage my brain and kill me. Hours later, when Dianne awoke, she would have waited for me to come out of the bathroom and called to me to see if I was okay. After a while, when I did not answer or come out, she would push the door open and would find me lying on the floor, dead. Fortunately, my head did not strike the wooden casings. Fortunately as well, my heart did not stop, which would also have resulted in my death long before I would have been found. Here was one of many times when the Lord preserved me when I could have, and normally would have, died.

During all of these horrible times, I tried not to show my family, or anyone else for that matter, how very miserable I felt. I could hardly stand the pain, the nausea, the vomiting, dry heaving, the difficulty breathing, the weakness and aches in every part of my body. I continually wrestled with the likelihood—actually the virtual certainty—that I would soon die. But I really did not want my family to suffer the torment of seeing how very poorly I was doing. It would not help me to feel any better, and it would only make them suffer more. But there were many times when it was very difficult, if even possible at all, to keep it from everyone, especially from Dianne and Craig. They were around me so much of the time, and I could not fully keep them from seeing much of what I was going through.

Just as had happened in 1991, around the time of my heart attacks and bypass surgery, for months I kept having thoughts planted in my mind that I should be angry with the Lord for what was happening to me. But the Lord was not causing it. What I was experiencing was not His fault. He was allowing it to happen. But I, like everyone else on Earth, was not supposed to be immune to sickness, pain or even death. All of those things are part of mortality, and mortality is part of Father in Heaven's great plan of salvation. His plan is for eternal happiness for me and all the rest of mankind. That eternal happiness and even glory could only follow one's faithful and obedient endurance of the trials that mortality would provide.

When the thoughts came to my mind that I did not deserve this and that it was not fair for me to be suffering through all this, I continued to remind myself of a number of things. Foremost was that someone far more worthy and undeserving of suffering than I—Jesus Christ—had suffered much more than I was suffering. During those times of my greatest suffering, I often read or recalled the verses of The Doctrine and Covenants, Section 122. They spoke of all kinds of trials and suffering that could come to the Prophet and that did come to the Lord. The verses then continued:

> . . . and above all, if the very jaws of hell shall gape open the mouth wide after thee, know thou, my son, that all these things shall give thee experience, and shall be for thy good.

Then comes the all-important lines:

> The Son of Man hath descended below them all.
> Art thou greater than he?[11]

I knew that I was not greater than He. If He was willing to suffer so much for me and for all mankind, being faithful to His Father, then I was willing to continue to be faithful to Him and to His Father and my Father in Heaven. The promise made to Joseph was, ". . . for God shall be with you forever and ever."[12]

I believed that this promise would be applicable to me as well if I would be faithful and obedient. I certainly believed that He could save me, even from an imminent death.

"But if not,"[13] I would remain faithful and obedient to Him. And whether I lived or died, I would still trust that He would be with me forever and ever.

CHAPTER TEN

MY HEART'S
LAST WEEK

It feels like one has been kicked
in the chest by a horse.

On the second Sunday of May 2004, we celebrated Mother's Day for my wife, Dianne. Two Sundays later, my family celebrated an early Father's Day, for it appeared unlikely that I would live to celebrate it on the third Sunday of June. My son, Craig, videotaped my wife and each of my daughters, and my only grandchild, Steven. Craig had his sister video his portion in the video he produced. Each of them talked to me, and spoke of things they loved and appreciated about me. It was a very moving and wonderful gift from my family to me, and a loving and deeply appreciated good-bye to me. Even today, this marvelous video tribute is one of my treasures. It still brings strong emotions whenever I review it.

Because my insurer, Altius Health Plans, refused to cover a heart transplant, my only options were to accept imminent death or find a way to pay for the procedure myself. On Friday, May 28, 2004, I met with hospital financial officials and asked them what it would take for me to be able to be put on the heart transplant list and receive a heart transplant. The response was that I would need to pay a specific number in the hundreds of thousands of dollars! They further informed me that I would need to make the payment of that amount in two installments of one-half the total each, with a specific time frame for making each installment. For me, it was a personal, frightening and discouraging time. For the men with whom I met, it was business. I suppose it could be no other way. I was nothing more than a paying customer.

I told them that I would come up with the money. I was driven back home, and, while continuing to decline in health, I began to come up with the way I would pay that huge amount to the hospital. Over the next two days, the Saturday and Sunday before Memorial Day, I individually and separately asked my wife and each of my children whether they thought it was worth it for me to come up with that large amount of money. I explained to each of them that should I do so, and if I still did not survive the transplant surgery, or if I only lived for a short time thereafter, it would be a horrible financial drain that Dianne and my children would be left to deal with after my death.

My wife and children all expressed their desire for me to receive the transplant if I could and have a chance to live, even with the risks I outlined to them. Their answers were predictable but very comforting and reassuring to me. Even when I pressed them with expressions of great risk and potential negative consequences, they persisted. If I could get a heart transplant, I should do whatever it took to do so. I should raise the money and pray for the Lord to enable me to live and have a successful transplant and recovery.

The next day, Monday, May 31st, was my daughter Becky's birthday and Memorial Day. Ever since the deaths of my parents, most of my brothers, sisters and I had gathered with our families at the graves of my parents to place flowers on Memorial Day. Then my family would go to a park for a picnic. On this May 31st, although I was doing extremely poorly, I wished to go to the cemetery to see my brothers and sisters and some nieces and nephews for perhaps the last time—to say good-bye—as my family all viewed it. My sister, Geniel, took a photograph of me that day in which I clearly look as if I am in my upper nineties, and not doing well for a person of that advanced age (See page 132.)

My immediate family and I did not go to the picnic after meeting at the cemetery, for my energy was depleted. Instead, my wife, children and I went home. While sitting around our kitchen table, my daughter, Emily, was seated at the opposite end of the table from me. During our conversation, she looked at me, and seeing that I appeared to be in pain, asked, "Are you doing okay, Dad?"

I shook my head and passed out. My heart had stopped. As I was collapsing onto the table, the bi-ventricular defibrillator fired, and I screamed and again passed out, but at least this time, my heart was beating. The reason I screamed was, no doubt, because of the painful feeling of the firing of the defibrillator. It feels like one has been kicked in the chest by a horse. The shock and pain caused me to again lose consciousness, even though my heart had been shocked back to beating.

My wife quickly rushed me to the hospital, and I, for the seventh time in under five months, was hospitalized in the Coronary Care Unit–4 North of the University of Utah Medical Center. The nurses there knew me. Many of them had cared for me on more than one occasion.

Wednesday, June 2nd, was my youngest daughter Emily's 18th birthday. Although I was not doing well, I appeared to be stable, so I was allowed to return home late that day, and I got to be with Emily on her birthday. I spent some time with her, sitting in the kitchen that evening. I asked her about her day and heard her tell of her day's activities. I got to wish her happy birthday and see the gifts she had received.

After only a short time together, Emily asked if I would mind if she went upstairs for a while, for she said she needed to do something. I would find out months later that what she needed was to be alone where she could cry, for she saw I was in so much pain that she could not bear to see it any longer. She expressed later that this was really the first time she had realized how much I was suffering. She simply could not bear to watch.

This was my firm desire, especially since they might very soon experience intense sorrow and suffering when I died.

In previous months, I had done my best to hide the pain I was experiencing from my wife and children, even though it was not always totally possible to do so. I had done a pretty good job most of the time. Even Emily, who lived in the same house, was at school most of the days and asleep at night, so she had not seen me at many of the worst times. I used up much of my energy trying to be with my family and to enjoy as much as was possible the time I spent with them. My efforts to appear free from pain when I was around them may have made me all the more fatigued. But it was important to me to have them feel as happy as possible whenever they were around me. They all had lives of their own to live. I wanted them to be able to live those lives as happily and easily as possible. This was my firm desire, especially since they might very soon experience intense sorrow and suffering when I died.

There were, of course, many times when I could not fully hide my suffering. There were times when I even needed to have Dianne and Craig help me to walk from my bedroom to the kitchen, or elsewhere.

"You need to come to the hospital and say 'Good-bye' to your dad."

On Thursday, June 3rd, the day after Emily's birthday, I had a very bad day. I could not keep down any food or drink. I was in increasing discomfort and pain. Finally, sometime after five o'clock, p.m., Dianne called the heart transplant on-call coordinator and told her that I was really not doing well. Although she had caught someone by phone, the nurse told her that the transplant office was closed. If Dianne felt I needed to be hospitalized, she should take me to the emergency room, and they would admit and send me to 4 North—the Coronary Care Unit. If I could make it through the night, then Dianne was told to bring me in at 9:00 a.m., on Friday. Although I continued to do very poorly, I did make it through that night.

On Friday, June 4, 2004, Dianne drove me to the hospital for my 9:00 a.m. appointment. I could not get myself out of the car, so she and a hospital employee lifted me out of the car and into a wheel chair. Once in the heart transplant clinic, I could not get myself out of the wheel chair, so the nurse dispensed with the normal procedure of weighing me, and instead wheeled me into an exam room. Dianne and the nurse lifted me out of the wheel chair and onto the exam table.

The physician's assistant, Kirk, came into the room to begin to examine me. I immediately lost consciousness, for I had gone into cardiac arrest. Kirk called out to me, "Glen, stay with me. Glen, stay with me." But I did not respond. The nurse quickly called out the door to broadcast code blue. I turned blue and began "to posture,"—which included my hands curling up, my eyes going back up in their sockets, etc. An extremely nice and personable nurse's assistant and a nurse coordinator of the transplant program quickly came in and began administering CPR to me. I later learned that LeAnn, one of the amazing coordinators of the Transplant Department, had only very recently completed the course that taught the latest techniques in resuscitating someone. Therefore, she was able to employ those most effective techniques to help revive me.

The hospital crash team responded to the code blue broadcast throughout the hospital. Since the exam room in which I lay was very small, the nurse had quickly ushered my wife out of the room and asked her to go back to the waiting area. Dianne left the room but stayed right outside the exam room door. She prayed aloud, "God, please don't let Glen die. God, please don't let Glen die." She then called our children at home and told them, "You need to come to the hospital and say good-bye to your dad."

The crash team descended on the heart transplant clinic and to my exam room, cut my shirt off, and placed the electrical paddles on my chest. The first shock did not get my heart started. Neither did the second shock, which used higher amperage. They followed normal procedure, turned up the amperage to a higher level still—the highest level they were supposed to use, and shocked my heart one last time.

Nearly fifteen minutes after going into cardiac arrest, my heart started and continued beating, but only very faintly. A strong medicine was injected directly into my heart. Though it was very good that my heart was again beating, it had been nearly fifteen minutes since my heart had stopped. Dianne was told there was a good chance that I would have some level of brain damage. I could even be brain dead. In fact, a few weeks later, we heard of a man in a neighboring county who went into cardiac arrest for eight minutes and was brain dead. There was real cause for concern.

They tried to get me as stable as possible, and then I was rushed to the cath lab, where a butterfly line was inserted into my neck and threaded down the vein to my heart so that this strong medicine could be pumped directly into my heart to help it keep beating. We were later told that when a heart goes into arrest and this strong medicine is used, either the heart, the liver or the kidneys, or any combination of them, can only handle receiving this medicine for hours or days, but normally not more than a week. Then the organs begin to shut down.

By the time I was taken to the cath lab, an operating room in the heart patient section, my children had arrived at the hospital. They were there at the cath lab when I was wheeled into it. One of the nurses there, seeing the deep worry on the faces of my children, loudly called out "Mr. Park!"

I opened my eyes, which my wife and children were able to see. That brought relief to their minds, for they saw that I was really alive and appeared to be better off than they had feared. At least I was not "gone." Knowing that my situation was very precarious and seeing the deep fear in their eyes, I was barely able to lift one hand and raise my thumb in a positive sign. I tried my best to smile "confidently." They really needed some encouragement and "lift" to ease their almost-overwhelming anxiety. Those little actions were all I could muster strength to do.

This day of my cardiac arrest was June 4, 2004, the day of the high school graduation of my youngest daughter, Emily. People often feel that a child is basically raised when she graduates from high school. My entire family were all painfully aware of the potentially ominous significance of this day. It could be said that all of my children were raised. If so, on that very day—to the very day—the Lord had kept His word, expressed in that priesthood blessing given more than thirteen years earlier. It could be said that I had lived to raise my children. So, to the very day, the Lord had, indeed, kept His word. But it appeared that it was not to continue for any time beyond that very day.

After I was taken into the cath lab, Dianne took our children into a nearby waiting room and closed the door. She recounted to them her experience of telling the Lord that she would accept His will, even if it meant that I would die. She expressed her testimony that it was so important for one be able to do that—accept the Lord's will over one's own will. Dianne asked them if they thought I should get a left ventricular assist device (LVAD) to keep me alive until a heart came available. They did not think I would live through that surgery. As they had each done when I had previously asked them, they told her that they wanted to do whatever it would take to have me get a heart transplant. Dianne then told our children that it would be wonderful if they could turn their will over to the Lord. She then asked if our children would each in turn, express their feelings, starting with our oldest child, Audrey.

One by one, they all expressed their hope and desire that I would live, that if it were necessary to come up with a lot of money, they thought we should do so. They also each declared their willingness to turn their will over to the Lord and to accept His will. They then all kneeled and my son, Craig, served as mouth for the family. He prayed that I might live, but told the Lord they all would accept the His will, even if it was that I should be taken.

During the prayer, the Transplant Department social worker opened the door. She saw my entire family kneeling in prayer and heard the faithful supplications being made. She quietly closed the door, impressed with the faithful actions of my dear wife and children. She is the same person with whom I had the short discussion in April about my faith in Jesus Christ and His love and support that gave me the strength to make it through all that was happening.

Following the prayer, Audrey said to her mother, "For all of these months, I have prayed so hard that Dad would live. I have never felt encouraged after any of my prayers. And now, I have told the Lord that it is okay if my Dad dies, and I feel okay. I feel such peace."

Without any question, the Lord had sent the Holy Ghost, the Comforter, to Audrey, to my other children and to my wife. He had brought that sure and real peace to Audrey and all of my family. That peace truly does surpass anything that the world could ever give. I am so grateful for the Lord's overwhelming goodness, love and grace that were given to them at this difficult time.

"Dad is going to live!"

A short time later, Emily forcefully expressed her hope and confidence by saying, "DAD IS GOING TO LIVE!"

After the butterfly line had been placed in my neck, I was moved back to 4 North—the Coronary Care Unit of the hospital. Emily, approached Dianne to tell her that she did not think she should go to her high school graduation commencement exercises that evening. Dianne told her that she thought she should go, and take a picture of me with her, and then I could be with her in that way and she could experience her graduation. Dianne told her that she was sure I would want her to go. So Emily decided she would do that, and hope that I would be okay until the next morning when she could visit the hospital again.

During the months before, I had helped Emily and her friends organize a senior trip to Newport Beach, California that was to begin the morning after graduation. I had lined up the house in which they would stay, the flights they would take, and many other details. I had collected the money from her friends' parents and paid it as a deposit on the home, and paid for flights and arranged for chaperones to go with them. Everything was in place.

Emily and her friends were scheduled to leave for California the next morning. But Emily did not dare leave. So her friends left without her. Emily did not know if I would still be alive when she returned from that week-long trip. So she stayed home, determining that she would miss her senior trip. Her friends expressed their hope that things would go well for me and left the next morning. I later found out that the following day, Sunday, those impressive friends had all fasted for me.

On that Friday night, my cardiologist, Dr. Gilbert, put my name on the Intermountain West Heart Transplant List in first position for my blood type. Federal regulations allow this for a person who is in extremely critical condition. But that positioning can only be for up to seven days. And then, if I had not received a transplant and was still alive, I would be moved back down to my chronological listing position—number twelve for my blood type in the Intermountain West region.

The next morning, Saturday, a blood draw was taken and it showed that my liver was not properly functioning, so I was removed from the transplant list. They will not waste a good heart on a bad liver. The first heart in more than two months came available later that day and I did not get it. Typically, when one is in such extremely critical condition, is receiving this strong medication and an organ ceases to function, it does not come back. But on Sunday, another blood draw was done, and the results showed my liver was again functioning! So at about 8:30 Sunday evening, Dr. Gilbert put my name back on the transplant list, again in first position. It was suggested to Dianne that it might be well for her to stay with me at the hospital that night, for I was not doing well. So she slept in my room.

"When the phone rang just after 3:30 a.m., my heart sank for I feared Mom was calling to tell us that Dad had died."

At 3:30 Monday morning, my nurse came into the room, awakened Dianne and said, "A heart's coming! A heart's coming! Dr. Gilbert is waiting on the phone for you!

Dianne hurried to the nurse's station and picked up the telephone.

Dr. Gilbert told Dianne the good news: "A heart is on its way. It will be here in an hour and a half."

Dianne's spirit leaped with joy. She immediately called our children at home to tell them the good news. Craig later spoke of his feelings. After having recently told the Lord it was okay if Dad die, Craig related, "When the phone rang just after 3:30 a.m., my heart sank for I feared Mom was calling to tell us that Dad had died."

Our receiving word of a heart coming for transplant in just seven hours after being put on the transplant list set a record for the Intermountain area. If it had not arrived so soon, I may not have lived long enough to get it.

At sometime before 5:00 a.m., I was wheeled into the operating room and was prepped for my life-saving, heart transplant surgery. My surgeon examined the heart I was to receive and, finding it in very good condition, my sternum was cut apart, my rib cage was opened and clamped to stay open. My coronary arteries and veins were connected to the heart-lung machine. This would keep blood flowing through my body. Then my heart was cut out of my chest cavity! A portion of my upper aorta was left in order to provide a solid base to which my borrowed heart could be attached. This would keep my new heart in place and not allow it to move around in my chest cavity. My arteries and veins were quickly sutured to those of this new heart. Everything else necessary was completed, the clamps were removed and my rib cage was closed. The two sides of my sternum were stapled and tied back together. My new heart was shocked to begin pumping again, and the skin of my chest was sutured back together. My condition was, and would remain for a period of days, extremely critical.

The surgery lasted approximately seven hours. That was agonizingly long for Dianne and our children. After it was finished, Dr. Karwandi, the surgeon who had also done the transplant the prior Saturday, came to the waiting room and told Dianne and our children that the surgery had gone successfully. Then he said, "The second heart was a better match for Mr. Park than the first would have been."

Prior to that second transplant—mine—no one on Earth knew that this would have been the case. Only the Lord knew that this second heart would be better for me. Just as He had done so many other times before, He allowed things to get worse and worse, until only He could save me, and then He would step in and do exactly that. Once again, things got about as bad as they could get.

He allowed my liver to cease functioning, and then He stepped in and saved me. It began functioning again. He knew that I would do better with the second heart, so He allowed my liver to cease functioning, saved someone else with the first, and then opened the way for me to receive a heart better fitted to me. It would enable me to do and experience that which He desired thereafter. The process of allowing this to come about was not an easy one for me or my family. No one thought it would go as it did. Faith was absolutely required if the miracle that was waiting would actually occur. A miracle definitely followed my faith, the faith of my family and that of our friends. There were friends of my children in multiple states whose faith and prayers likewise helped bring about this and other miracles. I believe that without that level of faith and the consent of the Lord, these miracles would never have occurred.

A little while after my transplant, I was told Dr. Karwandi had written that the heart I had received was in pristine condition. There was no evidence of any plaque build-up in the coronary arteries.

I will repeat what to me is so amazing that it borders, if not surpasses, unbelievable. I had actually gone through the process of dying. I had, in fact, died at the hospital. Incredibly dedicated and competent medical professionals brought me back to life, but my life continued to teeter toward permanent death (however weird that term may sound.) Then, after a two-month drought of heart transplants in the Intermountain West, I failed to get the heart that became available the next day. My liver ceased to function, which made me ineligible to receive that heart. But then my liver started functioning again—an unlikely occurrence. I was placed on the transplant list again and eight and a half hours later, I received a heart that was a better fit for me than the one I did not earlier receive. I received a second opportunity to live and to be with my family— borrowed from its original and future owner.

I am told that as I was being wheeled past my family on the way to receive the transplant, I grinned—kind of—and raised my hand. I dropped one finger at a time until only one remained up. They were so worried. They needed some reassurance. That was the best I could do to try to give them some—however small that was.

I know of nothing that I experienced the rest of that day, Monday, June 7, 2004. I only know that I received a second chance for life—a heart I borrowed from someone I did not know on Earth. Perhaps we were acquainted before mortality. I intend to be hereafter.

CHAPTER ELEVEN

BORROWED HEART

"That explains it."

On Tuesday, the day following my transplant, I regained consciousness. I was so frightened that I did not want Dianne to leave the room. In fact, I wanted her to sit as close to me as she could get. When she temporarily left her chair for only minutes, I panicked until she returned.

That day, I tried to express myself to Dianne. I said, "I feel—, I feel—," but I could not finish the sentence. Dianne could see the concern in the expression on my face.

She waited, and when I could not say more, she asked if I wanted her to give me a pen and paper so I could write it down. I nodded. She gave me a paper and pen.

I wrote on it for some time before I returned the paper to Dianne. She attempted to read what I had written, but to her dismay, it was nothing but scribbling! "Oh, no! Maybe he does have brain damage!" she thought.

To cover her worry, she told me that she did not have her glasses, so she couldn't read it. "Could you read it to me?" she asked. She handed the paper back to me.

Of course, I could not read it. I had not been able to say it in the first place! And that was only half of the problem. It was not real writing at all. I cannot remember whether I could tell that it was only scribbling or not. I simply accepted with frustration that I could not express myself.

For the rest of the day, Dianne would have to deal with the worry that I did have brain damage. As she would later state, "I knew it would drive Glen crazy if his brain did not function right, if he was not able to think and do the things he had always been able to do so well."

On Wednesday morning, I awoke and was really conscious and quite alert. Dianne and a nurse coordinator stood at the foot of my bed and told me several extremely interesting things. Dianne said, "You know what? You received a heart transplant."

I answered, "I did?"

"Oh yes. You got a heart transplant on Monday, two days ago."

"Wow," I responded.

"And do you know what else?" she questioned.

I shook my head.

"You received a woman's heart."

"Really?"

"Yes, you got the heart of a woman."

I immediately answered, "That explains it."

"Explains what?" Dianne asked.

"Ever since I awoke, I've had this uncontrollable obsession to go shopping!"

Dianne and the coordinator laughed. It was the first time in a long time that Dianne really felt like laughing.

The nurse coordinator and Dianne then enthusiastically added to my being told of the heart transplant, "Yeah, now you have everything–you have a woman's heart!"

I responded, "That's right. I do have everything—I have a woman's heart and a man's brain!"

That response seemed to end the conversation, or at least that part of the conversation. I wonder why?

Dianne then proceeded to explain to me many of the details about what she knew of my receiving the heart just two days before, including the statement by my transplant surgeon immediately following the surgery.

During our talk that morning, I told Dianne that I could feel that my hands, arms, feet and legs were getting greater blood flow. I had multiple tubes coming into and from my body and I was strongly medicated. But I could already feel so distinctly the difference from before my transplant.

My body was certainly not in good shape. Plus, my new heart had gone through so much trauma of its own, so it was not functioning as well as it would thereafter. This new heart had been shocked, while still in its original owner's body, to stop its beating. Then it had been held by a surgeon as it was cut out of its original body. Obviously, cutting off all of its connections to that body involved moving it upward, away from the body, and turning it from side to side to allow the surgeon to cut each coronary artery and vein that pumped blood to, and returned blood from, all areas of the body. Finally, even its aorta was severed from the body.

That surgeon, holding the removed heart in his hands, examined it carefully, turning it around and looking at its front, back, top and bottom. The heart was then put in a cold organ preservation solution and placed it in an ice-filled cooler to be transported to its ultimate destination—my body. A courier carried or pulled the cooler—certainly with some bumpy motion—both up and down and side-to-side—to an awaiting helicopter. It was flown from the other state's hospital to an awaiting jet. First, the courier got out of the helicopter, hurried to the jet and quickly climbed up the stairs. I wonder how much shaking and bumping the heart received in this and subsequent transportation transfers. The jet flew to Salt Lake City International Airport. The courier carried the cooler out of the plane and hurried to another helicopter. He jumped in, put the cooler down and buckled up. The helicopter carried the heart-laden cooler to the helipad outside my hospital. The courier got out of the helicopter, picked up the cooler and hurriedly proceeded into the hospital, down several halls and up to where the transplant team was waiting. My surgeon opened the cooler and removed the heart. He turned it over, examining it to see that it appeared healthy enough to proceed with the transplant. Included in his examination was checking out the condition of the inside of its arteries and veins. Even then, this borrowed heart's trauma was not over. The surgeon sutured its aorta onto the portion of my original aorta that had been left in my body for that purpose. Then all of this new heart's arteries and veins were quickly sutured onto mine. Even those on the back of the heart had to be connected to some of my arteries and veins. Undoubtedly, that required extra handling—trauma to that new heart. Finally, the heart had to be shocked into action—beating— once again. Often times, it is necessary for the surgeon to squeeze or massage it to help it start beating. No wonder it was not doing as well as it once had or as it would thereafter do.

Notwithstanding all of the above, it was so easily apparent that my extremities were getting great blood flow. They felt so much better than they felt during the many months before my transplant when my hands, arms, feet and legs ached day and night for lack of adequate oxygen and nutrients.

"I don't think . . . they will take the heart back out."

During that same Wednesday morning, Dianne dropped the bombshell she had just received from one of the main guys in the hospital's finance department. They wanted the full amount I was supposed to pay for the transplant by Friday, two days from then! After my meeting with the finance guys, a week before going into cardiac arrest, my health deteriorated far more rapidly than I or anyone else ever dreamed it would. When I received the heart transplant, the date when the first half payment was to be due had not yet arrived. So, obviously, I had not yet paid any of the total the hospital people demanded to be paid if I was to receive a transplant. They now demanded it—not just the first half payment, but the entire amount—and in two days to boot!

My first comment to Dianne was, "I don't think that if we fail to come up with it by Friday they will take the heart back out."

I then requested that Dianne ask my surgical ICU nurse if she could bring a telephone to my bed. Dianne asked her and the nurse brought a telephone to my bed and plugged it into a jack on the wall.

I called my son, Craig, and asked him to write down some things. While still lying in my bed, hooked up to wires and tubes galore, some 48 hours after my heart transplant, I dictated to him from memory multiple account numbers and other information for him to do in order to obtain the funds I needed to pay the hospital. Dianne was so relieved—she knew I was back. I must not have brain damage! I would never have been able to dictate so many numbers, etc., from memory with no prompting or notes. I did not even have any time to think it all through. I could not have dictated all of that if my mind and memory were not functioning well. Dianne silently said a relieved prayer of gratitude to the Lord.

As she did each time I was in the hospital, Dianne spent the entire day with me, and the same the next day, Thursday. When she came in Friday morning, she handed me a cashier's check payable to the University of Utah Hospital for the entire required amount and a receipt that Craig had prepared according to my directions for the guy in the finance department to sign. Since he had moved the due date for both payments dramatically ahead of the original due date of first payment, I was not going to allow there to be any possibility that he might claim he had not received the entire amount he had demanded. He was only doing his job. Expecting to receive it all four days after the transplant still seemed overly aggressive.

For all others—so many others at the hospital—I cannot express how grateful I really was, and still am. During my ten days in the Surgical ICU, I expressed my gratitude to my incredible cardiologist, Dr. Gilbert for everything he had done. His actions had helped save my life. He had done much for me for a long time before June ever arrived. His long and late hours, early morning follow-through, putting my name on the transplant list that Friday night, and then again going through all of the hassle and paperwork necessary to put me back on the list on Sunday. Those efforts had opened the way for me to get this heart and this chance to live— again. In short, those efforts had done so much to save and extend my life.

His answer was short and self-deprecating. "I was just doing my job."

I responded, "Well you certainly did it extremely well. But I still can't say how grateful I am."

I really cannot express how grateful I still am. I had received a heart transplant, and my cardiologist and the other cardiologists who had assisted me, the two amazing coordinators, both extremely capable nurses, the physician's assistant, social worker, pharmaceutical doctor, surgeon, his assistants, surgical nurses, technicians and the many nurses and nurse assistants who for years, and especially for nearly six months that year alone, had been simply marvelous and wonderful in every way to me. Not only had they saved my life, but they had made me feel as though it was their privilege and honor to do so much for me.

"... there are two types of spirits."

Many people have asked whether, during the nearly fifteen minutes I was in cardiac arrest, I had seen a light, or had some other "near-death experience." My answer has consistently been, "I do not remember most of what was going on at that time. But I do know without any question that there are two types of spirits."

After a transplant, a certain medication is given by I.V. to help keep the heart beating. A nurse monitors as the level is reduced over a period of 24 hours. Then, that medication is totally removed. The nurse monitoring this critical time carefully watches to see that the transplanted heart continues beating on its own.

Dianne remembers being told that when the flow of medication was stopped, my heart ceased beating. Shortly thereafter, it began beating once again, now on its own.

I later realized that as this critical moment approached, Satan, or one of his henchmen confronted me in his most hideously frightening form and told me that if I would simply relax and choose to let myself die, everything would be easy and pleasant—even wonderful. However, if I chose to live, he would make certain that my life would be miserable, painful and worthless. He gruffly demanded that I choose the easy and pleasant way.

Then, when my heart stopped, my spirit actually did leave my body. At this point, I looked at myself as my spirit stood slightly above and behind my head so I could see the top of my head, my forehead and face. I could also look at the front (top) of the rest of my body, legs and feet, covered by the sheet on my hospital bed.

It took several moments, at least, for me to realize what was happening. I was actually looking at my own body, lying on the bed. It was now obvious to me that my spirit had left my body. It seemed surreal—for it actually was. I wondered what was going to happen next. Would my spirit remain outside of my body? Was this the end of my mortal life?

The concern I was beginning to feel ended almost as quickly as it started, for there in front of me, instead of again seeing that monstrous spirit being, I looked upon two marvelous and wonderful beings who had been sent from the Lord. Spirits having authority from the Lord are always more powerful than those of Lucifer and his spirit followers. Unless a person makes the conscious choice to continue to communicate with, or to be influenced by, an evil spirit—which would result in the righteous spirit departing—the evil spirit will be driven away by the righteous one. The two opposite types of spirits cannot—will not—stay together in the presence of the other.

These two God-sent spirits were exactly opposite from the evil one. They did not audibly speak, but clearly conveyed their love and concern for me. They did not threaten and tempt me to end my life, simply by my choosing that option and ceasing to fight to live. These righteous spirits came to reassure, comfort and encourage me.

I cannot find mortal words to adequately describe this heavenly feeling and experience. My best attempt would be to say that I basked in a wonderful, refreshing and uplifting feeling—almost atmosphere, as it were—that was truly heavenly. All of my care was gone. There was, in their presence, nothing to fear.

These beings smiled a proud, loving and encouraging smile. As I looked upon their shining countenances, with surprise, I realized that these two beings were my parents! They were younger than I remembered them, which explains why it took several moments for me to recognize them. Again, the sweetness of the experience was such a lift and blessing. Although their visit was very short, their message was certainly sufficient and strong. I would be permitted—blessed—to continue to live a trial-filled, yet productive and love-filled life. After delivering their inaudible, yet unmistakable message, they simply departed. I remained there and pondered the wonder of what I had just experienced. I do not remember the process, but shortly after they departed, my spirit re-entered my body.

In my book *Our Next Life: A View into the Spirit World*, I provide quotations and elaborate on glorious descriptions of what awaits the righteous in the spirit world. I know the Lord to be so very gracious and loving. I had already made the decision, as I had expressed in hundreds of prayers, that I wished to be blessed to continue to live. I wonder if the Lord, in answer to my prayers, spared me—both when I was in cardiac arrest for nearly fifteen minutes and when my spirit left my body following the heart transplant—from the "temptation" I might feel to turn from that earnest desire to remain with my family after personally seeing all that awaited my eventual entry into that marvelous realm.

I continue today to marvel at what I felt and undeniably learned. Life continues after mortality. God is aware of each of His spirit children. When it fits His loving plan, He can and will send messengers to support and assist one of His children on Earth. He often will send someone who knows and loves the person still in mortality to deliver the message His wishes to convey.

I still cherish and ponder several amazing things about that experience. (1) I am thrilled and so appreciative to my Father in Heaven for allowing—directing—it to happen in answer to my prayers to Him for help. (2) I am grateful that the Lord Jesus Christ would cause it to occur. (3) I am amazed to have been blessed to both see and remember what happened. (4) I am impressed by how much information and how many feelings were conveyed in a short time, without any audible words being spoken. It was more like thoughts and impressions were being conveyed from their spirits to mine. (5) I am moved by **what** and **how** I felt. (6) I am amazed at how wonderful I felt then and still feel as I remember the experience.

Speaking of such ministering angels (spirits), President Joseph F. Smith said:

> In like manner our fathers and mothers, brothers, sisters and friends who have passed away from this earth, having been faithful, and worthy to enjoy these rights and privileges, may have a mission given them to visit their relatives and friends upon the earth again, bringing from the divine Presence messages of love, or warning, or reproof and instruction, to those whom they had learned to love in the flesh.[14]

"I am so proud of you."

After that experience, I really was revived. Dianne told me of what she and our children had done in the waiting room while the butterfly line was being put into my neck and threaded down to my heart. She told me, as I have written herein above, that each of them had turned their will over to the Lord and told Him that they would accept His will without being angry or resentful.

To Dianne and to each of my children, I said something like:

> I am so proud of you. When the chips were really down, and it seemed that exactly what you wanted so badly to happen was not going to happen—that the Lord was not going to grant your wish—you showed Him He could still depend on you. You proved to Him that you would still be faithful to Him. That is so important.

> It is much more important than my living. But now, we have it all. Not only do I get to live, perhaps for another fifteen years or more, but the Lord knows that He can rely on you. Thank you so much. I am so very proud of you.

I am told that during the first two days following the transplant surgery, I did some uncharacteristically bold and silly things. To Dr. Gilbert, I apparently performed a song, whistling two notes at a time in harmony. He seemed to be impressed and entertained—or at least amused.

Speaking of being entertained, I also sang to others, including my wife and children the song, "Let Me Entertain You," although I am sure that I don't now even know all of the lyrics!

The first few times I was helped out of my bed, I could only stand—with assistance—for twenty or thirty seconds. Then my legs (and maybe the rest of me as well) would give out, and I had to sit on the edge of the bed, and then be assisted in lying back down. Everyone who goes through major surgery has a difficult time standing and walking for a period of time following the surgery. Mine had been one of the most major of surgeries. And before the surgery, I had literally gone through the process of dying. None of the organs, muscles or cells of my body had received adequate blood flow, and hence, sufficient oxygen or the nutrients they needed. This severe deprivation had lasted for many months, and to some extent, for many years before that. There had been insufficient blood flow, if not severe blood and oxygen deprivation, to all of my body.

I had lost virtually all of my muscle mass. My arms and legs were basically skin and bones. I found, and years later still see, that my legs were the last major part of my body to "come back" to some semblance of normal strength. For months, even years, my legs remained so much weaker than they had been before 2004. For approximately a year, it was simply impossible for me to squat down and then rise back up without the assistance of either someone or something else. Even with such assistance, at first—and for many weeks—I had a very difficult time even standing up from a sitting position.

Each time I would walk with someone from cardiac rehabilitation, they would measure my heart rate and my blood-gas (oxygen) level. It was amazing that after a few days, my blood-oxygen level, the percentage of oxygen in my blood, was actually higher than that of the well-exercised and healthy man who was helping me walk! This was amazing! It gave me such hope.

Remember my recitation of the trauma my new heart had gone through. Nevertheless, this heart was working so well, despite the great trauma it had been forced to experience. In addition to going through everything I just described, this new heart had to operate with hostile blood cells which, if not for being bombed with immune system suppressants, would attack it as a foreign object— even a lethal enemy. My body was earnestly trying to isolate and kill the heart so that it would be unable to "harm" the very body it was keeping alive. That thought is so ironic. They, my cells, wanted to isolate my second heart so it would not be able to harm them and the rest of the very body that it is enabling to continue living a healthy life—one much healthier than they had lived for years.

CHAPTER TWELVE

RENEWED LIFE

"The wind beneath my wings."

While in the surgical I.C.U., each morning sometime between 3:30 and 5:00, a technician would come in and do a chest x-ray. Then, not too long after that, whether I was asleep or not, a resident physician would come into my room, check my chart and my vitals, ask me some questions, make notes on my chart and leave.

Each morning, a man would come in to collect the trash from two receptacles in my room. He always walked with his face turned down, never looking up, never making eye contact, never saying a word. After one or two days, when I noticed him enter the room, I would say, "Hi." Then, as he was about to leave the room, I said, "Thank you."

It took several days before he started looking up as I greeted him. When I greeted him as he entered the room, he answered, "Hi" back to me. When I told him "Thank you," he responded.

In not very long, when he entered my room, he looked right up at me and was ready to respond to my greeting. Likewise, when he would leave, he either said "Goodbye" or "You're welcome." He seemed to have gone from believing I would feel that he was not good enough to acknowledge, to appearing to feel that he was welcome and appreciated by me. It must have felt good to him. I know it felt good to me. And it was so very easy for me to do.

I am reminded of the account of a U. S. Navy pilot who survived as a prisoner of war in Vietnam for a number of years.

Charles Plumb was a U. S. Navy jet pilot in Vietnam. After 75 combat missions, his plane was destroyed by a surface-to-air missile. Plumb ejected and parachuted behind enemy lines. He was captured and spent 6 years in a communist Vietnamese prison. He survived the ordeal and now lectures on lessons learned from that experience!

One day, when Plumb and his wife were sitting in a restaurant, a man at another table came up and said, "You're Plumb! You flew jet fighters in Vietnam from the aircraft carrier Kitty Hawk. You were shot down!"

"How in the world did you know that?" asked Plumb.

"I packed your parachute," the man replied.

Plumb gasped in surprise and gratitude. The man pumped his hand and said, "I guess it worked!"

Plumb assured him, "It sure did. If your chute hadn't worked, I wouldn't be here today."

Plumb couldn't sleep that night, thinking about that man. Plumb said:

> I kept wondering what he had looked like in
> a Navy uniform: a white hat; a bib in the back; and
> bell-bottom trousers. I wonder how many times I

might have seen him and not even said, "Good morning, how are you?" or anything because, you see, I was a fighter pilot and he was just a sailor.

Plumb thought of the many hours the sailor had spent at a long wooden table in the bowels of the ship, carefully weaving the shrouds and folding the silks of each chute, holding in his hands each time the fate of someone he didn't know.

Now, Plumb asks his audience, "Who's packing your parachute?" Everyone has someone who provides what they need to make it through the day. He also points out that he needed many kinds of parachutes when his plane was shot down over enemy territory—he needed his physical parachute, his mental parachute, his emotional parachute, and his spiritual parachute. He called on all these supports before finally reaching safety.[15]

Sometimes in the daily challenges life gives us, we miss what is really important. We may fail to say hello, please, thank you, congratulate someone on something wonderful that has happened to them, give a compliment, or just do something nice.

This garbage pick-up man may not have been someone "important" in the world's eyes. But in God's eyes, he was as important as I, and he may have even been a better person than I was. Even if not, he was still a child of God. That alone, in reality, makes him important.

That account also brings up another terribly important point. How many people during the previous short period of time had packed my parachute? Oh my goodness! There had been so many: Dr. Fowles, Dr. Dodi, Dr. Ridges, Dr. Renlund, Dr. Taylor, Dr. Bouti, Dr. Gilbert, Dr. Bader, Dr. Karwande and many other doctors. Then, there were LeAnn Stomas and Shirley Belleville, those fantastic coordinators of the Heart Transplant Program and their predecessors. Kirk, the physician's assistant; Jason, the pharmaceutical doctor and Angela, the social worker, had all helped me. There were so many other competent and caring nurses, nurse assistants and others at the hospital. Then we come to my family, friends, neighbors and even friends of my family, some of whom I did not even personally know.

The most important of the mortal "packers" were my sweet wife, my son and my daughters. I could accurately describe them not only as packers of my parachute—but as Bette Midler sang, "the wind beneath my wings," that helped keep me from crashing.

At first and often, it hurt a great deal.

Every day in the surgical ICU, I pondered over and over in my mind the things I had experienced and the great blessings I had been given by the Lord. I thought of the opportunities that lay ahead. And I continually poured out my feelings of deep gratitude to Him for His mercy, goodness and love.

My time in the surgical ICU was not worry free or easy. Having gone through the surgery and being on the heart-lung machine, my lungs had fluid and phlegm built up in them. It was necessary that I breathe in hard and fast on a little breathing machine designed to allow the patient to force as large a quantity of air into the lungs as fast as possible. Doing so hurt. At first, and often, it hurt a great deal. The coughing that always followed also hurt, not just in my lungs, but in my not-yet-fused sternum. The coughing served a very important purpose. I coughed up fluid and phlegm from my lungs. I was supposed to do this breathing exercise five or six times each day, with multiple repetitions each time. It very soon became an exercise to be dreaded, for the pain and difficulty were always there. But it was essential that it be done—multiple times every day. That necessity did not end when I left the hospital. I had to continue to do these breathing exercises for weeks after my release.

Walking was both a nice diversion, but very difficult to do. I pushed myself to continually increase the distance and shorten the time it took me to go every individual distance. The fact that I was able to walk farther and faster than I was able to do such a short time before was greatly encouraging. I was determined to get stronger and to recover from the process of dying and from the surgery and trauma to my body and my new heart. I was determined to once again do at least most of the things I had always done with my family—now that I had this extended life. So I continued to push myself to do all of the things necessary to regain strength and vitality.

While in surgical ICU, I was told of a man in the room next door who was dying. He was going through horrible pain and problems following surgery to remove his tongue due to his smoking and chewing tobacco since he was a teen, as well as from other self-imposed health problems. It did not matter to me that he brought most, if not all, of his problems upon himself through wrong choices. I just ached inside for him. I found myself praying fervently for him, that his suffering might be decreased and that, if possible, he could be healed.

My tears and sincere supplication for this poor man were repeated multiple times every day. In addition to feeling deep concern for him, whenever I heard the medical evacuation helicopter flying out and then back in, I found myself in tears and in serious prayer for the Lord to bless and save the individual or individuals in need of that helicopter.

Every morning, I tried to hurry through the preliminary things I needed to do to get ready for the day. Each morning, these things hurt, but were necessary, and I would look forward to their being done and to having Dianne return for the bulk of the day. Although the day would be filled with activities that hurt as I pushed myself to do more, I knew that the result of my efforts would be a better, longer life.

In addition to doing my painful breathing exercises, I also took a number of walks each day. Every time I wished to sit up or get up, I had to call for assistance, for I could not use my stomach or back muscles to do so. Since my chest had been cut open, to do so would pull on each side of my chest. This would bring immediate and excruciating pain that was almost more than I could bear.

As I was being lifted up, I would carefully try to turn my legs so they would fall over the edge of the bed. Then, with further assistance, I would step down either onto a stool and then down to the floor, or eventually, directly onto the floor. Then I would be helped to stand up straight, and with someone on either side of me, holding onto me under my arms, I would walk out of my room and down the hall.

After a few days, I was able to take my walks with only one person assisting me. I was making progress! It was encouraging. Every day, I looked for any encouraging thing I could find. Some days, it was necessary to search diligently. But I was able to find something and hopefully multiple things every day. These encouraging accomplishments did not need to be big, but each was always significant—to me. Whenever possible, I found many things that I used to encourage myself and keep myself positive.

At one point, LeAnn, one of the coordinators, sat down and went over numerous things with me. She explained many of the things I would need to do following my release from the hospital. Among other things, according to my memory, she said something like this:

In receiving a heart transplant, you exchange
coronary artery disease for immuno-suppressive disease.

Things will not be easy nor without problems now that you have received a heart transplant.

The medicines you must take for the rest of your life will each have multiple side effects. It will be necessary to monitor you and the levels of these medicines in your blood from here on out. You will almost certainly have problems that will come up because of what you have already gone through, and as a result of the medicines and treatment you will hereafter receive.

We will follow up with you on a regular basis. You will have repeated biopsies done to see that your body does not reject your heart. And when any rejections occur, we will aggressively treat them with medicines that will also have side effects. It will not be easy, but we will stay very close to you to help make things as good as they can be. You will become almost like family to us, for we will see you and talk with you regularly and often.

We strongly recommend that you stay away from other people, except your immediate family—and then, only if they are healthy—for the next six months.

Transplant recipients who follow this counsel tend to live fifteen years, on average. Those who do not follow it tend to live about two years.

As the years have passed since my transplant, I have found her counsel to be absolutely correct. I have lived through complications, rejections, numerous side effects and additional illnesses. But I have also been enabled to live through wonderful, interesting and exciting times with my family.

CHAPTER THIRTEEN

A LIFE WITH
PROMISE

Once again, I had a life—one with promise
and not only pain and despair.

For the better part of the last two days before being released
after receiving my heart transplant, I was transferred from the
surgical I.C.U. to 4 North, the Coronary Care Unit, where I had
cumulatively spent nearly two months in my multiple hospitalizations
during the previous five months.

From there, my walks were longer than they had been. And
they included going to what we called "the bridge," a hallway
between two sections of the hospital. This hallway had windows on
both sides. Those on the east side allowed me to look at the foothills
and mountain above the hospital. The windows on the west allowed

me a view of the northern part of the Salt Lake Valley. It felt so good to be able to look outside at some of nature's beauty and the valley I knew and loved so well. It helped me realize that I really was alive and that I was going to continue to live and enjoy additional life with my family. As yet, I did not know what that life would be like. There would be many new and unpleasant aspects that apply to a heart transplant recipient. But my life promised to be wonderful—so much better than the prior six months had been. And the promise included that it may well continue for years to come.

Lying in my bed in this private room, I could look out the window facing south and see just the end of the mountains that circled around the southeast part of the valley. It was such a wonderful sight to see some of the mountains I had seen and loved all of my life. I simply cannot describe the exhilaration I felt. Tears came to my eyes a number of times during those two days as I saw this beautiful sight and realized that I would soon leave the confines of the hospital and be able to walk out-of-doors again. I would be able to see all of the mountains that surround this valley that was my home—mountains that were so impressive and beautiful to me. Once again, I had a life—one with promise and not only pain and despair.

There in 4 North, I could have visitors—well—only from people who worked in the hospital, in addition to my immediate family. I really did receive visits!

In fact, from fairly early in the morning until evening each day, I had a steady stream of visitors. In addition to Dianne and my children, my visitors included many people who had played important roles in preserving and extending my life.

Apparently, I was fairly well known to many of the nurses who had worked in the C.C.U. during the prior six months. Many of the nurses who had assisted and worked with me in my difficult times came to visit me on those days. Sometimes, it was just one at a time. Often, there were two or three in my room at a time. Some stayed up to an hour talking with me. One person, or one set of individuals would stay and talk for quite some time until someone else came in, and then the first would wish me well, say "Goodbye" and leave.

One special nurse even gave me a hug. She was a sweet, newly-married young woman, one who I would have been proud to claim as a daughter. She remembered how I had looked before the heart transplant. She was amazed at how good I now looked. In fact, she told me, "On that Friday when you went into cardiac arrest, I heard the 'Code Blue' broadcast throughout the hospital. I wondered if that was Mr. Park."

Everyone who visited me wanted to hear about the story of the prior two weeks. In our conversations, I told each the story of what had happened to me. I was able to express my gratitude to them for all they had done for me, and for the kindness and care they had given me. They all told me of the impressions they had had when they were working with me during my various hospitalizations. Generally, their expectations had been that I was on a fast track downward in the final stages of heart failure, a track that virtually always ended with cardiac arrest and death.

Most of them took the opportunity to give me some compliment for being a patient who tried to be in a good mood even when I felt miserable. They expressed sincere concern for me and they all showed their amazement at what I had been through and how marvelous the outcome now was. It really felt like these were special friends, even though I had not been around most of them for more than a couple of days each. That is, I may have a particular nurse for one ten-hour shift, but I was not her only patient during that shift. Some of them had been my nurse only once. Others had helped me two or three times. So, all told, for most of them, I may have actually been in their presence, adding up all of the seconds and minutes in one, two or three shifts, from less than an hour to less than three hours. But we had such a wonderful relationship because of their caring attitudes. The appreciation I felt for them was beyond my ability to express in words. In this setting, I nonetheless had a great opportunity to try to do so, despite my lack of adequate words.

I tried my very best to express my deeply-held feelings to these wonderful individuals—mortal angels—as far as I am concerned.

One of these visitors was the same social worker with whom I had discussed my faith in Christ and the same one who had walked into the waiting room to see my family kneeling in prayer together for my sake. In our long and wonderful conversation, she said, "Talking with you, hearing of your faith and seeing your family's actions have been a life-changing experience for me." There was a wonderful spirit present in the room during our talk that day. In fact, there was a non-stop wonderful spirit and feeling both of those days in 4 North.

"I can feel that!"

Before leaving the hospital, I had the first of what would be a multitude of biopsies. In this procedure, I lie on the operating table in the cath lab, being conscious throughout the procedure. After being prepped, I would turn my head as far to the left as I could. The doctor would shoot the right side of my neck with Lidocaine to numb the skin and the flesh right below it, and then proceed to cut into my neck. As the doctor cut into my neck, it really hurt! I could feel the scalpel cut the skin of my neck. In several biopsies, I called out, "I can feel that!"

The doctor ordered another shot of Lidocaine. And then he proceeded again. Several times, even that extra shot was not enough. I still felt the sharp pain as he cut into my neck. Another shot was given, and the procedure finally proceeded. He cut into the right jugular vein of my neck and "threaded" a sheath—a plastic tube—down the vein. Down in my chest, as the vein turned to the left toward my heart, the sheath hit the curve in the vein and it hurt. But the cardiologist continued to try to get the sheath to pass beyond that curve. After several tries—and still hitting against the curve in the vein—he finally succeeded and then he continued to push the sheath toward the heart. When the sheath hit the suture line where my vein was sewn to the corresponding vein of my borrowed heart, it was always very painful. This is an extremely delicate and tender part inside of my body—inside my chest. To have something hard and unyielding hit there is painful. On multiple occasions, during multiple biopsies, the same pain occurred each and every time in these same places. Each time after the first, I prayed so diligently and sincerely that the biopsy would be easy and successful. I prayed that the results would not show any rejection of my heart by my body. I prayed the sheath would not hit and be stuck, continually hitting that suture line. The Lidocaine only deadened the pain at and barely below the surface of the skin in my neck. Everything below that was soft, tender tissue that was being invaded, hit, and hurt, by unnatural, hard surgical instruments.

In each biopsy, after threading the sheath through the vein, the doctor inserted little snippers of a sort—attached at the end of a wire-like instrument with little handles on the upper end, somewhat like scissors. When the snippers were next to the inside of the heart, the doctor snipped an extremely small piece of the heart. Then he pulled the snippers out and dropped the little piece into a container. For the first few biopsies, the cardiologist repeated this for a total of four tiny pieces of the heart. After the first several biopsies, the number of snipped pieces was reduced to three. That was the number harvested during each biopsy for the next three years.

When the number of pieces of heart needed were recovered, the sheath was withdrawn from my neck, and firm pressure applied on the site of the incision to stop the bleeding. A bandage was placed on the site, and as needed, additional pressure was applied. Once, rather than stopping, the bleeding continued and pressure had to be applied for nearly forty-five minutes. A hematoma under the skin of my neck was one of the results. Another consequence was a huge, sore bruise that took weeks to heal and to quit hurting.

As I lay on the operating table during each biopsy, I could hear the heart monitor's "Beep, . . . beep, . . . beep." There was nearly a second between each "beep," for my heart rate was around 58 beats per minute. However, each time the doctor snipped off a piece of my heart, I heard, "Beep, beep, beep, beep, beep!" Approximately five "beeps" quickly rang out—all in about a single second's time. My new heart immediately reacted to the sharp pain it felt as a piece of its flesh was cut off. Then, moments later, it returned to a more normal heart rate and the monitor to the slower "Beep, . . . beep, . . . beep." When the next snip happened, the same response and sounds occurred. Since there was no nerve connection between this new heart and my brain, although the heart definitely felt the pain, my brain did not receive the message and I sensed no pain. I felt sorry for this poor borrowed heart, for it definitely did sense the pain.

I had a biopsy performed once per week for the first two months following my transplant. Then, for the next several months, I had a biopsy every other week. Then it was once a month for several more months, followed by one every other month. The results of the early morning biopsy usually would be received by the Transplant Department late that same day, or the following morning. I would then receive a call from one of the coordinators to give me the results.

At one appointment, Shirley, a coordinator, suggested that it might help if I would eat some pizza for dinner the night before the biopsy, for the larger-than-normal salt content would serve to dilate my veins, including the interior jugular vein. This could make it easier for the sheath to move down, around the curve, and past the suture line into my heart. It seemed to work. The next biopsy was easier and less painful than any of the prior ones had been. So the dilation of the vein allowed the sheath to slip a little more easily and less painfully to my heart. Thereafter, every time, the night before a biopsy, I ate pizza. That was about the only time I would eat it. It certainly served its purpose.

I am still amazed that eating something with extra salt would make that much difference in the small veins in a human body. It makes it easier for me to believe that what we eat can have a profound effect upon us and the organs and blood vessels in our bodies.

CHAPTER FOURTEEN

RETURN TO NORMAL LIFE-- ALMOST

Possible/Likely Side Effects--A Multitude

I was discharged from the hospital late in the morning of June 16, 2004. During the ride home with Dianne, I felt in awe and experienced such joy in once again seeing the Salt Lake Valley and its lovely sights. I was so grateful that I was alive and able to see these places again. I was even happier that I was going to be with Dianne and our children in better health than I had experienced for some time. Moreover, the potential was that this opportunity would last for years. As I walked in the door of our home, I was overcome with joy and appreciation for the blessing of life and being with my wife and family once more. My home looked so good. It was so wonderful to be there.

Within a short time that first day back home, I spent about forty-five minutes reading through a legal document. Dianne scolded me, saying, "You shouldn't be worrying about doing legal work now. You just got home from a heart transplant!"

I answered, "It feels so good to be able to focus on something besides surviving."

It really did feel good to have my mind able to think about something else, knowing that I would likely be able to focus on many other things for years to come.

Now home, I began following a strict regimen of taking many medications at various times and days. I had seventeen different types of medications. That does not mean I had seventeen pills to take. Some of the seventeen medications involved taking more than a single pill—eighteen of one—for that particular medicine. And, I had to take some of them twice each day. Each one had its own side effects. Many had multiple and potentially serious side effects. Some of them had the same potential effects as others. Some had their own unique side effects. The following is a list of side effects and the number of medications that could cause each of them:

Possible/Likely Side Effect	Number of Medications With This Side Effect
Abdominal pain	5
Agitation	1
Allergic reaction	1
Anemia	1
Anxiety	1
Bleeding gums	1
Blistered or swollen skin	1
Bloating	1

Possible/Likely Side Effect	Number of Medications With This Side Effect
Bloody or black-colored bowel movements	2
Blurred vision	1
Bone pain	1
Brittle bones	1
Cancer	2
Cataracts	1
Chest pain	2
Chills	1
Chubby cheeks, neck	1
Closing of the throat	2
Confusion	1
Constant hunger	1
Constipation	3
Continued thirst	1
Cough	2
Declining kidney function	1
Diarrhea	3
Difficulty breathing	4
Dizziness	5
Dry mouth	1
Fainting	1
Fatigue	2
Fever or chills	2
Fever or other signs of infection	2
Flu-like symptoms	2
Frequent urination	1
Gas	2
General feeling of discomfort	1
Greater susceptibility to infection	2
Hallucination	1
Headache	6

Possible/Likely Side Effect	Number of Medications With This Side Effect
Heartburn	1
High blood sugars	1
Hives	2
Increased nose bleeds	1
Risk of developing lymph node, or other tumors	2
Insomnia	4
Irregular heartbeat	2
Loss of appetite	2
Mental/mood changes	2
Metallic taste	1
Muscle pain or tenderness	2
Muscle weakness	2
Nausea	5
Night sweats	1
Numbness or tingling of the hands or feet	1
Organ rejection problems in transplant patient:	1
Painful urination	1
Paleness	1
Seizures	1
Serious birth defects to children of men, women taking	1
Severely low levels of red and white blood cells and platelets	1
Shortness of breath	1
Skin changes	1
Skin growths	1
Skin rash	4
Sore on the skin that feels warm/tender/painful	1
Sore throat	4
Swelling of hands, throat	1
Swelling of the eyes or eyelids	2
Swelling of the feet or lower legs	3

Possible/Likely Side Effect	Number of Medications With This Side Effect
Swelling of the gums	1
Swelling of the lips, tongue or face	3
Tightness in the chest	1
Tremor	2
Ulcers	1
Unusual bruising or bleeding	3
Vision changes	2
Vomit that looks like coffee grounds	2
Vomiting	4
Water retention	1
Weakness	4
Weight loss	1
Yellow skin or eyes	1

Note these additional warnings from my medicines:

"This medicine may cause cancer; Others should avoid touching the tablets; Avoid contact with broken or crushed tablets; Do not throw any tablets in the garbage or down the drain; If the capsule should come apart, avoid inhaling the powder and avoid direct contact with the skin or mucus membranes; If contact should occur, wash thoroughly with soap and water; rinse eyes with plain water."

As toxic as these warnings sound, these are the medications I continue to take.

It is a fun list, don't you think?

CHAPTER FIFTEEN

BEFORE AND AFTER

From ninety-three, plus, to fifty-three

Each day following the transplant, Dr. Gilbert came to check on me. One day as he walked into my surgical I.C.U. room with one of the coordinators., he said, "You look ten years younger today!"

I responded, "So now I look like I'm only in my upper 80."

We both chuckled and went on talking.

Dr. Gilbert checked my vitals, asked me how I felt and I asked him my questions.

The truth was that if I looked like I was ten years younger, I would indeed look as though I was now in my eighties.

I continued, "If I keep getting ten years younger each day when you come in, I'll soon look like I'm a teenager. Then I will look at Dianne and say, 'Look at me, a teenager and I'm married to a fifty-three-year-old woman!'"

Dianne, who was also in the room, loved my remarks, of course. We all laughed. Dianne seemed to laugh with a little less enthusiasm than the rest of us.

It was true that I was looking younger each day. The obvious reason was that my entire body was getting very good blood flow. The parts of my body that had been deprived of adequate blood flow—every single part—had aged many times the normal rate. Now every part of me was getting good nutrient- and oxygen-filled blood. Interestingly, my body was now actually going through an extremely fast process of undoing the premature and rapid aging that had taken months—even years—to do.

The photographs of me on the following pages tell an incredible story of the process I just described. One interesting thing about these photos is that the "before" looks as though it should be the "after" and vice-versa. But they appear in the proper order. The older-looking guy is me—one week BEFORE my heart transplant. The younger-looking guy is also me—four weeks AFTER my heart transplant. Therefore, the transformation you see took place in five weeks! Actually, I began to look much like the "after" photo some time before the four weeks had passed.

Photo taken one week BEFORE my heart transplant.

Photo taken four weeks AFTER my heart transplant.

"I am becoming more and more thin-skinned."

In August 2004, two months after I received this wonderful transplanted gift, the biopsy results, as usual, came later in the day. The results, however, were not as usual. They showed that my body was rejecting the heart. It was a mid-level rejection. These words from the coordinator hit me like a brick.

"What does that mean?" I asked.

"Well, we're going to need to have you come to the hospital. We will need to hit the rejection with some medicines to get this rejection stopped."

So Dianne took me back to the hospital, where I would stay for the next three days. Again, I was bombed with medicine—primarily prednisone, a corticosteroid. There was a woman who had received her transplant three years earlier who had never had a rejection. She and I sat in the waiting room of the cath lab that morning, and my biopsy occurred right after hers. But we both had our first rejection discovered that day. She and I were both hospitalized that same night.

There was no comfort in someone else also having a rejection. In fact, it was just the opposite. I now realized that it was possible that I could go for a long time, and still end up having my body reject this new heart. That was not comforting at all.

One of the side effects of prednisone, especially at higher dosages, was that I would balloon up in several places—my face, my neck, both front and back, and in my stomach. It increases the load placed upon my liver to process it out of my body. It also makes the skin become thinner. Thinner skin makes it easier to sunburn, bruise, scratch and bleed.

At one appointment with Dr. Gilbert, I joked, "I don't want you to tell anyone, but by taking this medication, I am becoming more and more thin-skinned."

His reply was something to the effect, "My wife would say I have that problem without taking any steroid!"

The truth is, after having to take that medicine for nearly two years, my skin has become thinner, not in any emotional or personality sense, but physiologically. And years later, it does not seem that any of the "thickness" has returned. Apparently, once thinned, the epidermal layers of the skin remain thinner.

I jokingly asked Dr. Gilbert, "Why does prednisone cause me to puff up here (I pointed to my stomach, neck and face), and not here (I flexed my bicep)?

He responded, "Prednisone is a corticosteroid, not an anabolic steroid. Prednisone suppresses your immune system, but anabolic steroids do not. They help build muscle mass, but have many serious side effects.

There were and are other side effects of the medicines I have taken. They include achy muscles, muscle cramps, head, neck and back aches, shakiness, trouble falling asleep, sleep interruption, diarrhea—and believe it or not, the opposite—constipation. These different effects come from different medicines that I must take together. Possible side effects can also include liver and/or kidney damage, and dramatically increased susceptibility to skin and other cancers. These medicines drain calcium out of my body, which must be replaced. I must be careful about my exposure to dust, spores found in soil and plants, all kinds of germs, fungus and bacteria about which most people really do not need to worry. About the only good restriction in activities in which I can be involved is that I cannot change diapers. What a sacrifice—one I'm willing to make!

After returning from the hospital following that first rejection, I continued to take a high dosage of prednisone, along with a new, different immuno-suppressant medication. Over time, that dosage of prednisone was decreased little-by-little, until nearly a year later, I finally ceased taking that essential—yet obnoxious—medicine, at least for the first time in more than twelve months.

Rejection is obviously a serious matter. It could accurately be called a deadly matter. In the case of a transplanted organ, the normal immune system response to such foreign matter within the body is to send certain types of cells to attack the foreign molecules (germs, bacteria and diseases—and the toxins they produce.) The body's lymphocytes—including B cells and T cells, antibodies, and other immune cells—attack these foreign molecules and tissues. Unfortunately for transplant recipients, the organ they received to save and extend their life is actually also the very foreign molecules and tissues that their body believes to be the enemy. Therefore, all of the body's immune system's forces attack and seek to isolate and kill that foreign "enemy." Only the effect of sufficient and well-balanced immuno-suppressant medications can prevent such rejection, attacks and death to the foreign, yet essential, organ. Also unfortunate is the fact that the suppression of the immune systems prevents the body from adequately fighting off real enemies—viruses, germs, bacteria, toxins and cancers.

So I went up, two stairs at a time.

When I received my discharge instructions ten days after my surgery, I was told that walking up stairs, with frequent rest, was an excellent exercise. When I returned to my home, I was determined to get stronger as fast as I reasonably could. So I thought that walking up the stairs in my home multiple times each day would be a good idea. I immediately found out what "frequent rest" meant. For weeks, it meant three or four rests while climbing a single flight of stairs! But I did not allow myself to get discouraged. I would climb three or four stairs and then rest for 20 to 60 seconds. Then I would climb another three or four stairs, rest again, and then continue in that way until I had climbed all sixteen stairs. Descending the stairs also required rests, but was obviously much easier than mounting them. I tried to climb and descend the stairs ten to fifteen times each day. Soon, I would climb six stairs, rest, then climb five more, rest and finish the last five stairs. Then it became climb seven, rest, climb five, rest, then climb four.

I was excited when I could do nine stairs before resting and then finish the last seven. The number of rests stated above does not count the rest I always took at the top of the stairs!

Each time I started climbing stairs or walking fast, I noticed that it took my new heart several seconds to "catch up" with the added need for oxygen my lungs and muscles were experiencing. Once it was pumping faster, it seemed capable of keeping up with my body's needs. I learned that I should begin breathing more deeply immediately before I started such increased physical activity. This helped to provide my lungs and muscles with some extra oxygen while they waited for my heart to get more oxygen flowing through its increased pumping.

As more time passed and my new, borrowed heart grew stronger and recovered from the trauma it had undergone, it seemed to me that it "learned" to respond somewhat faster to my body's increased activity. It did not begin pumping fast as quickly as my original heart had when it was healthy and strong. But it did start to respond to my body's greater needs more quickly than it originally had.

All of my adult life, whenever possible, I have gone up stairs two at a time. But I could not now—at least not until sometime in mid-October—four months after my transplant surgery. By then, I had for some time been able to climb all sixteen steps without a rest—until I was at the top. Then I decided that the time had finally come for me to try going up the stairs two at a time! I had planned this for a few weeks. I was going to pick a time when I felt strong and well, when Dianne was in the house but was not watching me. She, therefore, would be close enough to hear me if I fell or otherwise needed her help but far enough away to not object to my trying it.

So I went up, two stairs at a time. Whew! When I reached the top stair, I was really tired. I rested and then fairly quickly I sat down to rest—to really rest—without my legs being required to support me. But I had done it! I will take you through my thought process. I had literally gone through the process of dying. All of my muscles had atrophied to virtual non-existence. I had even died, fortunately, where I could be resuscitated, and more fortunately, with miraculous intervention from the Lord, I had been given a second chance to live. I now had a strong heart that had been transplanted in my chest. I was, only four months earlier, unable to stand on my own, unable to walk, and now, I had just climbed an entire flight of stairs, two at a time, with no help!

In addition to climbing stairs, I walked each morning and evening, from one end of the house to the other, over and over again. I started walking for three minutes each morning and three minutes each evening. That may sound pathetically short. But I had no muscles or strength. It was actually quite tiring. After the first few days, I increased my walks to four and a half minutes morning and evening. Then four days later, I increased them to six minutes, twice a day. After three or four weeks, I began going to rehabilitation at a building near the hospital. The first time at rehab, the nurse asked me if I thought I could handle walking at a slow pace on the treadmill for ten minutes. I responded that I should be able to handle that, "for I am walking twenty minutes each morning and evening every day at home."

The nurse, startled, said, "Do you think you should be doing that much?"

"Well," I said, "I have been slowly increasing the time every few days and have made sure that I never let myself get feeling too fatigued."

She appeared reassured, and I proceeded to walk for ten minutes. One normally would not increase the time every four days. The usual regimen for heart patients calls for increasing the walking time by about 15% every seven days. I was motivated to move faster if I possibly could do so. And I did.

"Glen is recovering well from his heart transplant surgery. But tonight is not about him. Tonight is Natalie's and Josh's night."

Only a few weeks after my transplant, my daughter, Natalie, married Josh Benson. Being quarantined, I could not attend the reception. That really made me sad, but she and everyone else understood. They were happy I was alive. We all knew we had a reasonable expectation that I would be around to share many happy and great times with them throughout their future life together.

Originally, they had scheduled their marriage for October 2004. Because of my failing health, they moved it up to August. Then, as my health began to deteriorate more rapidly, they moved it up to July 10th, for they wanted me to still be here, if possible, when it happened. Poor Natalie had to do almost everything in the arrangements for the wedding, for Dianne was so busy taking care of me and being with me before and after my transplant. Dianne spent as much time as possible helping Natalie, but she was unable to do as much for Natalie as she has been able to do for our other children.

We welcomed Josh to our family. At the reception, my son stood in for me, standing next to Dianne. My family had earlier taken a photograph of me, a copy of which is included on page 133 herein above. Dianne had it enlarged and placed on an easel with a message I wrote that stated, "Glen is recovering well from his heart transplant surgery. But tonight is not about him. Tonight is Natalie's and Josh's night."

The reception went well. Natalie and Josh took off on their honeymoon. Dianne and my family returned home that evening to find me well at home. I later had the opportunity to watch a video taken of the evening.

I knew it from direct communication
of the Holy Spirit to my spirit.

For the weeks after I returned home from the hospital, every morning and evening, and also during the day, I prayed sincerely, expressing my deep gratitude to my Father for the great blessings I had received. I knew with certainty that the Lord had saved my life—my earthly life. No one could have persuaded me otherwise. I absolutely knew this was true.

One night, after praying, I fell asleep and awakened during the night and got up to go to the bathroom. The only things on my mind were these: (1) I needed to go to the bathroom; (2) I must be very careful getting out of bed—my sternum was not yet fused together, and it will hurt a great deal if I twist my body at all; and (3) I need to be quiet so I don't awaken Dianne.

While I was walking to the bathroom, with my mind focused on being quiet, the Spirit spoke to me, "The Lord saved your life." I could not contain my emotions. It was such an overpowering experience. I already knew that the Lord had saved my life. In fact, no one could ever have convinced me otherwise. I thought before that wonderful experience that I knew it as well as was possible to know it. But now, I knew it in a way that was beyond my prior knowledge. I knew it beyond man's own ability to know. I knew it from direct communication of the Holy Spirit to my spirit.

"Does Glen have cabin fever . . . ?"

Following my release from the hospital, I was virtually quarantined for six months. My nurse coordinators counseled me to stay away from anyone except my immediate family for a period of six months. I should not go to church, restaurants, stores,—basically anywhere—except to my appointments at the hospital. I remembered the above-written statistics of those who follow their counsel, on average, about fifteen years. Those who do not tend to live about two."

With those vastly different lengths of life expectancy, the decision was easy to make. In fact, there was really no contest. I had not fought so hard to live, just to throw it away. So I stayed away from everyone for the next six months following my transplant. To some who might be offended by my standoffishness, I explained, "It's not that your germs are necessarily worse than mine. My body is just not used to yours."

Extended family members and friends asked Dianne and my children, "Does Glen have cabin fever from not being able to get out and do normal things? They responded, "No, he is happy. He always keeps his mind busy. He is always doing something. He doesn't let himself have time to get discouraged."

Every day I followed a productive and interesting schedule. After awakening, I prayed. I did my walking and breathing exercises.

Then I showered and shaved. I ate breakfast. Then I studied the scriptures and other material I was researching. I wrote in one or more of the five books I was writing.

Before 2004, I had begun writing three books, all religious in nature. While I was in surgical I.C.U., I had asked my nurse for a pen and some paper, which she provided, and I wrote out ideas about work, about things I wanted to do, and books I wanted to write. I outlined some of the books I wanted to write and some things I wanted to add to the books I had already begun. Upon returning home, with the potential of living for much longer, I started to complete those plans. Within the next few months, I finished my already-started research for most of the five books I was working on. On my 54ᵗʰ birthday, October 30, 2004, I signed the applications for five certificates of copyright on the books I had finished by that time. I mailed in the applications and manuscripts to the Copyright Office in Washington, D.C. Two of those books are already published: *Our Next Life—A View Into the Spirit World*; and *What Satan Doesn't Want You To Know*. The other three are in final revision. In addition, I have published two additional, political books.

I continued to outline additional books I wanted to write and also began writing some of those additional books that I intend to hereafter complete.

At the end of December, my quarantine was over. It felt so good when I was able to return to church and the temple. It is definitely not a situation where I got out of the habit of going to church, or of wondering if I wanted to return. The fact was I could hardly wait to go back to church. I really wanted to be there. It was not a duty but a joy to go to church once again.

". . . if you want a Chateau Brian, have a Chateau Brian. If you want a milkshake, have a milkshake."

When I was about to leave the hospital, Dr. Gilbert counseled me about many things. Among other things, he said, "I want you to gain fifteen pounds as fast as you can. Normally, we tell patients to avoid certain types of food. But for the next while, I want you to eat anything that looks or sounds good. In other words, if you want a Chateau Brian, have a Chateau Brian. If you want a milkshake, have a milkshake."

I took his advice—immediately. When I was told that Emily was coming that afternoon to visit me in the 4 North Coronary Care Unit of the hospital, I called and asked her to get some cash from my wallet, and take a small cooler with some blue ice packs, a plastic cup and dish towels to Iceberg, a fast food restaurant that specializes in thick and tasty shakes. I asked her to get two things—a Philadelphia and Swiss steak sandwich and a cherry, chocolate chip, banana shake! The cooler with blue ice packs would keep the shake from melting. The extra cup was for the part of the shake above the rim. The dish towels were to fill in around the ice packs, to keep the shake from tipping over. Emily bounded into my hospital room and handed me the delicious, non-hospital, food. They tasted so good. I thought, "I'm going to enjoy following Dr. Gilbert's advice."

The fact is, I enjoyed eating—everything. Everything tasted wonderful. The appetite I once had—and then lost—had returned. With a good, strong and functioning heart, my stomach, my digestive system and even my taste buds had all returned to good—even great—working condition. It was so nice to be able to once again eat and have things taste good. It was also so nice to be able to keep everything down after I had finished eating!

All of my life, I have loved chocolate cake and milk. When I was growing up, my mother baked 10-12 loaves of homemade bread every other day. She also baked a large, flat chocolate cake—usually twice a week! I loved both of them. And I ate a lot of both.

On a normal school day, I ate the breakfast my mother made, and then for dessert, I would have some chocolate cake and milk. In my lunch, Mom would generally add a piece of chocolate cake for dessert. When I got home, my after-school snack was chocolate cake and milk. My dessert at dinnertime was chocolate cake and milk. And guess what my snack at night before going to bed was almost all of the time? Right—it was chocolate cake and milk. My favorite chocolate cake was the recipe my mother had always made.

When my family gave Dianne and me a couples' shower before we got married, we received various recipes to give Dianne some good ideas for various types of food. One of those was the recipe for making the same type of chocolate cake my mother had made. What a great idea! So the cake Dianne has generally made for me all of our married life has been my favorite chocolate cake. I never grew tired of it. I still prefer it today.

During the first half of 2004, everything went wrong in my body. As I have related, it was at the time of the three-month period of vomiting and dry-heaving that most things changed. Remember my Valentine's Day chocolate cake. After only one bite, I could not eat any more. I put it away, thought about it for a couple of days and could not bring myself to eat any more of it. Even the thought of actually eating any almost made me sick. So I asked Dianne to put it in the freezer for me, hoping that the time would come when I could again stand to eat my favorite dessert. The time did not come until after my transplant—months later.

Soon after I returned home, I saw that everything looked and tasted very good. So I took the cake out of the freezer and had a piece. It tasted so good. It felt wonderful to feel like my normal life was coming back—at least many parts of it. The coming was not necessarily fast. I had a great deal from which to come back. I had literally gone through the process of dying. Every part of me: every organ, system and cell of my body had suffered for a long period of time from woefully insufficient oxygen-rich blood flow. The muscles throughout my body had deteriorated to virtually nothing. My curly hair had almost all turned white and gone straight. I had gone to the point of being virtually unable to walk, sleep or breathe. My liver had ceased functioning. And for nearly fifteen minutes, no part of me had blood flow, or even life.

CHAPTER SIXTEEN

MARVELOUS CREATION

"The body has a backup system."

After having had several biopsies, I asked one of my coordinators some questions, including: "I know that when I received my heart transplant, my original heart was cut out of my body and removed. In doing so, all nerves were severed, and when my new heart was sewn in, the doctors' efforts were to secure this new heart to a portion of my original aorta, and then to quickly suture coronary arteries and veins that came with that new heart to my arteries and veins. But there would not have been any attempt to connect any nerves of my body to those of that new heart. And I

147

know that my new heart feels when pieces of it are cut off during my biopsies. The heart feels it, but I do not, for the signals of pain that the heart is sending out never make it to my brain, for there is no nerve connection between the two. So, what tells my new heart when it needs to speed up or do more?"

The coordinator replied:

> That is a good question. The body has a backup system. Normally, the brain sends commands or instructions via the nerves to the heart, and it responds. Without that connection, the brain sends its command and the body sends hormones to the heart to get it to speed up.

This helped explain the delay in my heart's response to climbing stairs or starting to walk fast. Still, there is a response. The heart did respond, nonetheless. The hormones took longer to "inform" the heart that it needed to pump faster so my lungs, muscles and other body parts could receive sufficient oxygen to handle the greater load being placed on them.

I was so impressed with the greatness and thoroughness of the Great Creator who had created the marvelous human body. It is really something for this to come about all by chance, the result of some Big Bang, out of nowhere! I write facetiously, for I do not believe for a moment that we got here on Earth with these extraordinary bodies without the involvement of an all-powerful and all-knowing Creator. Actually I wrote the facetious sentence above to show how very ludicrous—ridiculous for anyone to believe—that the marvelous human body came about without the actions of that all-knowing Creator. A watch could not—would not—come about without someone making it. But compared to a mere watch, the human body with its amazing brain, organs and systems, is billions of times greater, more complex and impressive that any watch will ever be. Plus, no watch will ever be able to reproduce its own kind.

My feelings are in contrast with those of many people. As to the human heart, they are also far different from the thought and impression of Dr. Christian Barnard, who, following the first heart transplant in 1967, said, "For me, the heart has always been an organ without any mystique attached to it . . . merely a primitive pump."[16] He obviously had not experienced the heightened sensitivity and emotion that follow having one's heart handled during heart surgery.

The heart's process of receiving and pumping blood may be simple in many respects. A scientist may consider it to be "primitive." The intricate functioning of its valves and the way its chambers—the atria and ventricles—expand and contract, is amazing. All of the chambers coordinate their contracting and expanding with the opening and closing of each valve. The coordinating of all of their movements with each other is also that of a superb and precise instrument. This precise coordination of contraction, expansion, opening and closing of valves allows blood to come from the body into one chamber, being held there by a closed valve. Then, just at the right split-second, that valve opens and the blood is pushed into the next chamber, a ventricle. A valve that holds the blood there opens, exactly as that chamber contracts, forcing the oxygen-deficient blood to the lungs. Incredibly, the blood somehow picks up oxygen and then flows back to a third chamber of the heart. Another closed valve suddenly opens and the blood is pushed by the same type of contraction into the fourth chamber, another ventricle. Finally, that ventricle's other valve opens as the ventricle contracts, and oxygen-rich blood is pushed through the body's arteries throughout the body. Additional valves exist even in the arteries and veins. These help the blood to continue flowing where the body needs to have it go as even the walls of the arteries contract in just the right way and at just the right time to accomplish this amazing process. This provides fuel the cells and muscles need to function.

Then, amazingly, the oxygen-depleted blood returns through veins to the hearts first chamber, an atrium, and the process begins all over. All this usually happens in about a second! The heart a primitive and simple pump? Absolutely not!

To me, I look upon the heart as a magnificent organ created by a supremely intelligent, all-knowing God. I will always believe that expressions to the contrary are the result of the arrogance of man's education and experience. Men and women, especially those who are in positions of power, or those who feel they control things that can mean the difference between life and death, can feel that they know and can do much more than they actually can. And being trained to divorce themselves from personal attachment or involvement in the emotions of physical problems, they often tend to look at physical things as simple objects to be analyzed and manipulated. Sometimes they are successful, and things continue to look simple to them. Other times, they are not successful, and those same simple things somehow became too complex for these "great controllers" to control or even effectively influence.

The greatest inventors and the finest surgeons have been unable to duplicate the amazing human heart. Every artificial heart has failed to adequately replace that "primitive pump" or to perform its functions in a way that served to extend the recipient's life for very long. And the quality of that short extension of life was so poor that it could hardly be properly called a true extension of life. Even the LVAD, which can often sustain life for some time, requires a large pump and power source to keep it operating. It is cumbersome and uncomfortable. So, to say it in other words, the "primitive" human "pump" does things that the greatest medical and inventive minds cannot duplicate.

To bluntly address that human opinion, I ask if these great medical minds cannot come close to duplicating its performance, how much less than primitive does that render these minds and their abilities, at least in comparison with the true Master's mind?

I dare to say that the human heart is a masterpiece and part of an even more fantastic masterpiece that was created by the real Master—God.

CHAPTER SEVENTEEN

WONDERFUL PEOPLE

. . . I realize more than ever before how many nice and wonderful people there are.

After going through these experiences, I realize more than ever before how many nice and wonderful people there are. So many people brought meals, treats, notes and letters of encouragement, and had prayed and fasted for me and my family. Some "angelic" neighbors brought meals for months. I know of my name being on the prayer rolls of numerous temples, inside and outside of Utah. Family members, both immediate and extended, friends, friends of my children, ward members, members of prior wards, and others had prayed continually for me. I have often said what I believe to be true at least in part—I was alive because of the faith and prayers of so many wonderful people. I wrote letters to some of my neighbors especially those with young children, taking the opportunity to express gratitude to them, and to bear my witness of the Lord and of His willingness to listen to and answer the prayers of His faithful followers. Clearly, their prayers in my behalf had been heard and answered.

"I have a letter from the donor family. Do you want to receive it?"

A little over five months following my transplant, I received a telephone call from the social worker in the Heart Transplant Department. She said, "I have a letter from the donor family. Do you want to receive it?"

"Of course," I answered.

She stated: "Okay. It has been reviewed by the social worker at the hospital where the donor heart was harvested, then reviewed by the person responsible at the Intermountain Transplant Association. I, too, then reviewed it. It does not give you any private information that you should not receive.

Within a couple of days, I received the letter. One of the children of my donor sent me a short letter to tell me a little about the wonderful woman whose heart I had received, and also a little about her family.

Because of the many hands through which it had to go, and perhaps because the letter had not been mailed immediately after it was written, I did not receive the letter written in September until November. Since it had already taken so long for me to receive it, I wanted to immediately respond, for I certainly did not want the donor family to believe that I did not think they were important enough for me to promptly respond. I immediately drafted my response to the touching letter I had received from a gracious person who had lost her loving mother in a tragic accident. This fine family had lost a loving wife, mother and grandmother. I considered this such an important letter, for I was writing to the family of the woman whose life was lost, and whose heart was now keeping me alive and was giving me the prospect of living for many years. The best way to state what I said is to include the letter itself in its entirety.

Dear Donor Family:

I just today received your letter dated September 21. I wanted to respond rapidly to your letter. Hopefully, the necessary process will get this letter to you soon. It was so nice to receive your letter and to hear you describe your special mother. I have assumed that she was a caring and loving person. I appreciate learning about some of her impressive qualities. And I am happy to know a little about your family. It sounds like a wonderful and close family. At a future day, I do look forward to meeting your mother and personally expressing my appreciation to her.

I am so sorry for your great loss. At least in some way, I can understand how deeply you feel about losing such a wonderful part of your life. I lost my father and mother while I was in high school. They died three and a half months apart from each other. I remember well the loss I felt.

I just had my 54th birthday. I thank you, your family and your mother that I had the opportunity to experience this with my family. My wife and I have six children, one grandson, and a granddaughter due in January. My oldest three have graduated from college. My three youngest daughters are currently in college. I am grateful that I can be here to help them while they are in school. My youngest daughter graduated from high school on the day I went into cardiac arrest. After a difficult weekend, I was the beneficiary of your mother's and your family's generous gift of life. Through the blessings of the Lord and the goodness and giving of your mother and your family, I have this second chance.

Thank you for your thoughts and prayers. Please know that from the time I was fully conscious following my surgery, I have prayed, asking for the Lord to buoy up and give His peace to the family of the wonderful person from whom I had received this precious heart, and to convey to her my deep appreciation. As grateful as I was and still am, I was immediately aware that my blessing came at incredible cost to another family. I hope you know that I firmly believe that no good person is taken before his or her time. The Lord, in His wisdom, knows of your mother's goodness. He undoubtedly has her involved in helping others and continuing her own progress on the other side of the veil. I know that she will feel great joy in doing so. There must be many, many there who are now the beneficiaries of her love and caring.

For many years, my family has designated themselves as organ donors and they donate blood regularly. Since I have been unable to do either, I have tried to help those in need in other ways. As your fine family continues your mother's legacy of caring and helping others, I will also try my best to add to that legacy by extending my efforts to help others, because I will now again be able to do so.

Again, thank you for your sweet letter, and for your family's goodness and fine example. Your mother and your wonderful family will always remain in my thoughts and prayers.

Sincerely, Your Friend

CHAPTER EIGHTEEN

A NEW ILLNESS

"I didn't know whether I would be able to get him to the hospital fast enough."

On January 6, 2005, my daughter, Audrey, had her second baby, and named her Emily. After her birth, Dianne and I flew up to see them. It was wonderful to get to see my second grandchild and my first granddaughter. Dianne and I stayed for several days and got to spend time with Audrey, David, my grandson Steven, as well as little Emily.

During our stay, I began to feel sick. Then I grew increasingly sicker. I immediately called and talked with Shirley in the Heart Transplant Department. She gave me instructions of what I should and should not do. At this point, there was some suspicion as to what it might be—at least on her part—not mine. But no one was sure yet. I started just lying around most all of the days, and I continued to get sicker.

Soon, I felt that if I was going to be able to make it home, I had better leave. So I flew home, while Dianne remained to continue helping Audrey with Steven and her new baby. At home, I continued to get worse.

Some days later, Dianne returned home. She found me so ill that she told a friend, "I didn't know whether or not I would be able to get him to the hospital fast enough."

She called ahead. When I arrived, a room awaited me in 4 North. I remained in sweat pants and shirt. They covered me with seven warm blankets. I know that it took more than an hour even with all of that, before I stopped shivering. They immediately put in an I. V. and began a dose of Valganciclovir. To my knowledge, that is the sole medication that will effectively treat the infection I had. I continued on this I. V. medication for several days. Then, in order to allow me to return home, I had a pique line installed in my arm, so I could still have the medicine flowing directly to my heart. At home, I received sufficient spheres full of the medicine for me to hook up to the pique line morning and evening for the next ten days. In this way, I could complete my treatment. At about the end of the two weeks of medication, I was over the human cytomegalovirus, HCMV, or CMV, infection and began what would be more than a month of recovery from that horrible experience.

My new heart had come with this virus. Since I had never had the virus during my lifetime, my body had never built up any antibodies for resistance against it. With my immune system being suppressed so that my body would not reject my heart, I could not build up any such natural resistance to it. So later in my renewed life, every time I would become very sick or rundown, this latent virus would flare up again into a life-threatening infection. Each time, it would cause me to become very ill and I would have to wait nearly two weeks in order to have it conclusively determined that I had the dangerous infection again. Then it would take an additional two weeks of treatment with the same medication to get control of the CMV. After that, I would take another month or so to recover and regain strength that I had lost during my fight against this lethal infection.

The possible consequences of CMV are as follows: gastrointestinal distress (the least serious), liver damage, then liver failure, kidney damage, then failure, followed by blindness and finally, death. Indeed, after I came home from my first bout with the infection flare-up, Dianne went to a shop that was run by two sisters she knew. When Dianne told them what I was going through, they told her, "Yeah, our father got a heart transplant. After three years, he developed CMV and died from it." So we had impressed upon our minds just how serious this thing really was.

CHAPTER NINETEEN

LIFE IS GOOD

The first day I went, the habit of regular
attendance was back in full force.

Beginning in January 2005, I was able to carefully return to church and to serve in the temple as I had done since 1982. My Bishop requested that members not shake my hand so I would not get any illness from anyone. Everyone was very careful around me.

It was so wonderful to be able to once again go to church and worship the Lord. On Fridays, I was able to return to the Jordan River Temple and serve in my calling there. I could not believe how great it felt to be able to return to both church and the temple.

Many people say they no longer go to church because they got out of the habit. I learned that this is only a part—actually nearly an irrelevant part of the story. When one, for whatever reason, ceases to go to church because of sin, or through, having lost the

Spirit—then it is possible to get out of the habit of going to church. But the habit is not just of going to church. It is of keeping the commandments, praying, studying the scriptures and seeking to retain the Spirit. When some of those habits are lost, the habit of going to church often ends as well.

For me, the habit of going to church after nearly a year of being unable to go was simple to re-establish. I wanted so badly to be able to go that when I was once again permitted to do so, it was with profound gratitude and joy that I returned. The first day I went, the habit of regular attendance was back in full force.

Our Body in the Resurrection

In the spring of 2005, one Sunday's Priesthood lesson from the *Teachings of Presidents of the Church: Wilford Woodruff* lesson manual was "Understanding Death and the Resurrection." The instructor had someone read the following quotation:

> It is comforting, at least to my spirit, to think, that, in the morning of the resurrection, my spirit will have the privilege of dwelling in the very same body that it occupied here. As elders of Israel we have travelled (sic) a great many thousand miles in weariness and fatigue, laboring to preach the gospel of Jesus Christ to the children of men. I would be very glad to have the same body in the

> resurrection with which I waded swamps, swam rivers
> and travelled (sic) and labored . . .[17]

After having these sentences read, the instructor paused and asked, "Does anyone have any comment about this quotation?"

This seemed an unusual place to stop for discussion, and no one raised a hand, so I did. I said: "I have a different perspective on this subject than anyone else in this room. I have learned that cells have memory. The person whose heart I received must have been a sweet-oholic. Prior to my heart transplant, other than having chocolate cake and milk, if I was given the opportunity to have either dessert or an additional serving of the main course, I would choose more of the main course. Sweets were generally something I could do without. When I received candy from my wife or children, I would put it in my home office. Very often, more than a year later, they would find it uneaten, usually unopened and going bad."

I explained that after my transplant, I could not get enough sweets. I wanted them all of the time. Before my transplant, I would only eat one cookie, even though I was offered multiple. After my transplant, I could eat several and like it. After a few months, I decided that I must gain control over this addition to my body. My spirit had to take control over this new part of my physical body.

This experience taught me that if I had to receive some other person's body in the resurrection, I would have to start all over to gain control over every single part of that body. I would have to gain control over every appetite of the flesh—including very literally the appetite for food. But all other desires and appetites that that body had acquired over a lifetime—an entire mortal lifetime—would have to be brought under the control of my spirit. I, too, am very grateful that I will receive in the resurrection the same body in which I preached the gospel, raised a family and experienced serious trials in mortality. I already have enough to do to bring my own body under the control of my spirit. I don't need anyone else's problems, appetites, passions or sins to contend with.

"What would you think about our working together again after I graduate?"

Craig had worked for me for two years prior to my heart transplant. During the last six months of those two years, in my business matters, he was my arms and legs, and often my voice. Dianne took care of most of my other needs. Craig and Dianne did so very much for me. Audrey, Becky, Natalie, Anne and Emily spent time with me and helped in every way they could. Audrey flew down from Washington State and literally spent months with me. Becky, Natalie, Anne and Emily left school, work and friends to spend time with me and to encourage me.

A year after my transplant, Craig was about to leave for Notre Dame to pursue his Master's Degree in Business Administration. About a week or so before he was to leave, all of a sudden, it appeared as if there were several things floating in my right eye and my vision was somewhat clouded. I immediately got an appointment with an ophthalmologist. While I was still in his office, he set up an appointment with an eye surgeon. He told me I had a detached retina and would need to immediately have surgery. If anything bad happened before I could have the surgery, I would lose sight in that eye. Until I could have that surgery two days later, he advised that I lie down as much as possible. When it was necessary to walk or stand, I should keep my head tilted to one side. This would keep the pressure and weight of the fluid in my inner eye from pulling the detached retina farther down, which would make me lose sight in that eye. With that as the consequence, I tried diligently to follow his directions.

I had the surgery, which the surgeon pronounced as successful, and I returned home. Following the surgery, I needed to keep my head tilted in the opposite direction. Now I needed to keep pressure on the re-attached retina so it would help keep the retina attached to the rest of my eye.

While I still had the bandage over my eye, I said good-bye to Craig as he drove off to South Bend, Indiana to begin the orientation and courses for his M.B.A. I was thrilled for him to be able to pursue this graduate degree, but at the same time, I was very sad to see him leave. He had remained with me for almost a year after my transplant to make sure that I was "back on my feet." Now he was gone and I felt a great loss. I fully supported his decision to continue his education. I knew he was certainly capable and deserving of this opportunity to pursue and obtain his Master's Degree. He would do well in Notre Dame's accelerated program. He would be a great influence on many people there. He would make many friends and serve as an example to them. My only sadness was losing his daily companionship and of not being able to regularly do things with him.

Fortunately, I continued to improve in health—with periodic lapses. About 45 days later, my whole family went to visit Craig. He came home after his first semester ended in August. Then Dianne and I flew back in October. Craig returned home for Christmas break, and then again for spring break in 2006.

Before the end of Craig's first semester, he emailed me to ask what I thought about his pursuing entrepreneurship as his emphasis. I responded, "If that is what interests you, then that is what I think you should do."

His next email asked, "What would you think about our working together again after I graduate?"

I replied, "I think that would be great." I felt that it would be great to work with such a fine, trustworthy and hard-working man.

When Dianne and I flew back to visit Craig that October, several of his friends from high school and college also went to spend some time with him. One evening, we all went to the clubhouse of his apartment complex and played three-on-three basketball. After a short time playing, Craig insisted that I sit down and rest. The other five continued to play without me. Not long after I had sat down, I stood up and got back into the game. Craig was very concerned about my overdoing. I was probably more concerned my team would find that they could win without me! I did sit out quite a while, but I also played—perhaps longer than I should have. Other than being fatigued, I noticed no other negative consequences.

The following May 2006, we rented a trailer and drove to South Bend, Indiana to help Craig move back after he had finished his intensive, three-semester degree. Then, after Craig and we all traveled for a while, he once again began working with me.

As the eye surgeon had predicted at the time of my retina surgery, a little more than a year after the surgery, I developed a cataract and required surgery to correct it. Again, I had a bandage on my right eye.

In August 2007, my youngest daughter, Emily, married Samuel Steele. This time, I was able to be involved in every part of the preparations, the marriage and reception. It was nice to be back to near-normal once again. We were happy to welcome Sam to our family.

"Well, we almost lost him today."

Every June following my heart transplant, I have an annual exam, which is comprised of a two-day battery of tests. The first day, usually a Monday, begins with a morning meeting with one of the two great coordinators of the Heart Transplant Department. There, the coordinator goes over a list of questions about my overall health and follows up on things I have done or had done to me during the year. The list includes, but is not limited to, dental exams, results of eye exams, results of appointments with a dermatologist, etc. On the second annual exam appointment, the coordinator asked me, "Have you had any cancer yet?"

"Yet?" I asked. Do you expect me to have already developed cancer?"

"As we explained before you left the hospital after receiving your transplant, one of the side effects of your immuno-suppressive medicines is to make you extremely susceptible to cancer—especially skin cancer. In fact, the leading cause of death in heart transplant recipients after the first year is cancer."

During my third annual exam, on the second day, the usual tests included a biopsy, an angiogram and right heart catheterization. During the angiogram, something happened, that I will explain later. But this significant occurrence was totally overshadowed by a serious complication that arose. During the procedure, the catheter hit the wall of a coronary artery, which caused the artery to flutter and then collapse. I immediately felt horrible and told the cardiologist who was performing the angiogram. But he already knew something was very wrong, for the heart monitor showed there was trouble. During these procedures, my head is covered with a sheet that is propped up so the sheet does not lay flat against my face. I have some breathing space and a very small space through which I can look to my left. This allows the doctor to have easy access to my right jugular vein.

A nurse was immediately next to me, talking to me and asking me if I was okay.

"I don't feel well," I answered.

As the doctor called out orders and activity in the room increased dramatically, this nurse remained right at my side, repeatedly asking, "How do you feel? Are you okay? How would you describe the pain, from one to ten, with ten being severe?"

I suspect that her constant questions and talking served three purposes—to actually find out how I was doing, to keep my mind occupied with our conversation and to see if I passed out. The fact was, I was not doing well at all. Every part of me—my entire body—hurt. I felt nauseous.

In order to get things going again, the doctor asked me some questions to determine what I could be given to help the situation, without having serious negative effects. By that I mean there were several medicines to which I had previously experienced severe negative reactions. A couple of these were medicines that would ordinarily be used to help get my heart beat back to normal. Since these could not be used, he asked, "How do you react to nitroglycerin?"

I wasn't quite sure. But something had to be done, and immediately. So I was quickly given one nitroglycerin pill and told, "Here, suck this under your tongue."

I did as I was told. My condition soon grew worse—very much worse.

The doctor called out additional orders. I was feeling worse and worse. The nurse continued to talk to me and to ask me how I was doing.

All of a sudden, she put two orange pads on my chest. I knew what they were used for. Nonetheless, I started to ask, "Why are you putting . . ." Before I could finish the sentence, I lost consciousness.

When my body was affected by the nitroglycerin, the same thing happened to me that had happened twice before. My blood pressure plummeted, down to about 50 over something. On March 28, 1991, I went into flash pulmonary edema, which brought on my third heart attack. After being rushed to a hospital, I was given valium in an effort to stop my heart attack. My blood pressure plummeted to that same dangerously low level and my doctors immediately stopped the valium flow and commenced something else in order to help increase my blood pressure.

Then on February 4, 2000, during the angiogram to determine if I needed a heart transplant, I was given valium, and my blood pressure also dropped to the same extremely low levels. Now, let us return to this third annual exam. After I lost consciousness, I went into cardiac arrest. Before I could fully die, electrical paddles were placed on the orange pads on my chest and my heart was shocked back to beating.

Dianne had dropped me off at the hospital early that morning and was to return to pick me up after my recovery from the angiogram and heart catheterization at about 1:00 p.m. Following my near-death and revival, I was wheeled into the recovery room. I asked the nurse in charge there to call Dianne and tell her that I would not be ready until later than we had originally thought. So she came about an hour and a half later to pick me up.

When Dianne arrived, the nurse in the recovery room greeted her with, "Well, we almost lost him today." All of a sudden, Dianne nearly panicked, for she had left me that morning and now realized that she had nearly lost me—again. The feelings of the absence of control and concern for how long I would be allowed to live returned in an instant.

Unfortunately, the cysts continued to grow.

After having had my new borrowed heart for more than three years, I was cleared to have a procedure done that had waited for at least nine years. Back in the late 1990s, my dentist told me that I had a cyst in both of my lower jaws that needed to be removed. The one in my right jaw was much larger and more serious. But my heart was doing poorly and my cardiologist felt it was not wise to try to have that surgery done then. Since the cysts were not life-threatening, I deferred having the surgery done. Unfortunately, the cysts continued to grow.

When I met with an oral surgeon in November 2007, his x-rays showed that the cyst in the right jaw had not only eaten away much of the soft tissue in my jaw, but it had penetrated the jaw bone. In fact, it had eaten away much of the jaw bone as well. My oral surgeon, Dr. Patrick Brain, told me he was very concerned that my jaw could break—not only during the surgery—but before surgery could even be done. He was worried it might break if I chewed on anything the least bit hard. So for the weeks during which I waited to have the cysts removed, I ate only soft foods and did not chew at all on the right side of my mouth. Dr. Brain conferred with some of his colleagues in Michigan about how best to deal with this very delicate situation.

A short time before I was to have oral surgery, I was pushing against a large fallen limb by standing with my left shoulder under it and my knees bent. I tried to lift the limb by trying to straighten my legs to stand up. The limb was far too heavy. I felt and heard something in my shoulder pop, and I felt immediate pain. Thereafter, if I tried to lift anything, even my left arm, the pain was intense. Two different doctors, an industrial accident/sports medicine specialist and an orthopedic surgeon, both initially diagnosed it as a likely torn rotator cuff. The rotator cuff is the network of four muscles and several tendons that form a covering around the top of the upper arm bone (humerus). If torn, it requires surgery. It would be important to not wait too long for the shoulder surgery so the muscles and tendons would not lose their elasticity. The surgery would require pulling the torn and separated pieces together and stapling them so they would remain connected. But it would be too much for me to go through two surgeries of this magnitude without some time separating the two. It was determined that I would proceed with the oral surgery, and then, hopefully, the shoulder surgery would follow, sometime after Christmas. I hoped my muscles and tendons would retain their elasticity until then. The pain was intense anytime I tried to even lift my left arm or move it away from my body. So I also hoped I could endure the pain that came numerous times every day for the next five weeks.

While all of my family went to St. George for the Thanksgiving holiday, I stayed home. There was no way I would be able to drive or ride so far, nor do any of the activities that would be going on during the trip. On the days while everyone was gone, I worked—doing paper work—very carefully. Whatever I would do, I was always at risk that something could happen that would result in my shoulder hurting intensely. I prayed so sincerely that things would work out well for both my shoulder and my jaws.

I have very fast reactions. Generally, these reactions are automatic, not even conscious. I can be sitting and peripherally see something falling off to my side. My arm will automatically shoot out to catch the falling object. I often succeed in catching it. With my shoulder injured, the result of that automatic reaction would not be pleasant.

I got a great deal accomplished during that solitary Thanksgiving vacation. After several days, I was sitting in a recliner, reviewing some papers. A paper felt off the left arm of my recliner. Without thinking, my left arm went out to grab the paper.

All of a sudden, I realized what had just happened—and not happened. My injured arm had gone out to my side without my even thinking about it. That was what had happened. What had not happened was that there had been no pain! I very carefully used my right arm to bring my left arm back to its safe position next to my body. Then I pondered that short set of events. After a minute, I again used my right arm to move my left arm into that previously-painful position and then lifted it back close to my body. I repeated the process. I again used my right arm to move my left arm into what had recently been another very painful position. Then I slowly let go with my right hand, ready to quickly grab my left arm if the pain returned. But it did not. I did not understand. The same motions and positions earlier that day, and for more than a week, would have brought great pain. But the pain was not there. Why? I am not certain as to the physical mechanics of the "why," but I got on my knees to express gratitude to the Lord for the blessing that had "mysteriously" come to me—for the spiritual "why."

During the next several days, I remained careful not to overdo anything. I did use my right arm to repeatedly move my left arm to positions that would keep my left arm limber and delicately exercised. As the days passed, my left arm continued to get even better. The pain also continued to diminish. I was so grateful.

I called the orthopedic surgeon and reported the change in my shoulder. No surgery would be required after all. Wow! What a relief. Whatever had been the problem with that injury, it was virtually gone. Unfortunately, the same was not the case with my jaws.

It still surprises me, even though it is a daily experience.

Finally, the day arrived for my oral surgery. After the operation was completed, my surgeon told me that it had gone quite well. He told me, "Your right jaw bone was paper thin in several places. The cyst had penetrated the bone in multiple places and had eaten away much of the bone."

Dr. Brain had removed both cysts and injected into my jaws a medication that would help kill any possible remaining particles of the cysts. This way, there would be a great chance that the cysts would never return. Lab results later would show the cysts were benign. Thank Goodness.

The two things about which my oral surgeon remained very concerned were these: First, for the next many months, my jaw could still easily break. It was still paper thin and did not even have the cyst to fill in the large gaps between the thin bone. So, for six months at a minimum, I would need to refrain from chewing on the right side of my mouth.

Second, the cyst had wrapped itself around a nerve in my jaw. The nerve was not the one that controlled movement in my jaw or lip. It was, however, one that controlled feeling in the right side of my lower lip, on down to the bottom of my chin on that side. Dr. Brain had tried very hard to remove all of the cyst without breaking my jaw and also without tearing the nerve.

He told me that it appeared he had been successful in the first, most important thing—my jaw, though paper thin—had not broken. Unfortunately, pieces of the sheath around the nerve had pulled away with the cyst. There would be an excellent chance that feeling would be lost from mid-lip to the right side of my lower lip, on down to the bottom of my chin, from middle to a point directly below the right corner of my lower lip.

To this date, that feeling has not returned in that area of my lip or chin. It still feels weird. When I touch it, it feels much like one's mouth feels when a dentist deadens it. Unlike when one's mouth is deadened, this time, the normal feeling does not return. When I have any pressure, even very slight, applied on the skin next to this numb area, there is a strange sensation. After several years, I still am not fully accustomed to that weird feeling. It still surprises me, even though it is a daily experience.

I was blessed to be able to be fully involved in both of these great occasions.

The year 2008 brought two wonderful events in my life and that of my family. In March, my daughter, Becky, married Joel Hemingway. He was a welcome addition to our family.

In August, my son, Craig, married Melissa Cannon. I was happy to welcome her to our family as my only daughter-in-law.

I was blessed to be able to be fully involved in both of these great occasions. Moreover, just as I had done with my three prior sons-in-law, I was immediately able to love these wonderful individuals who became part of my family.

"I felt that!"

I now return to that which was overshadowed during the dramatic day of my third annual exam when my heart stopped. It occurred again the following year during my fourth annual exam. During the biopsy of my fourth annual exam, when the cardiologist doing the procedure snipped a piece from my heart, I jumped and called out, "I felt that!"

Twice more, he cut off little pieces of my borrowed heart. Twice more, I felt the pain my borrowed heart experienced when parts of it were cut off!

The cardiologist completed the biopsy and I was sent to have an echo-cardiogram. Later, I met with one of my cardiologists, who talked with me about my test results. Our talk included what I had felt during the biopsy. My doctor stated that a small percentage of heart transplant patients begin to regain feeling in their heart—their transplanted heart! Somehow, nerves were fusing, re-establishing at least some connection between the heart and the brain. Again, I was simply amazed at the complexity and marvelous nature of the human body God created.

The regenerative powers of this incredible creation were wonderful—even miraculous.

CHAPTER TWENTY

NARROWING ONCE AGAIN

The very medications that are keeping me alive are also killing me!

During the angiogram in my eighth annual examination, I had a bad news—good news—bad news—good news—bad news—good news experience. The angiogram showed a 90% blockage in my circumflex coronary artery. A stent was needed to open the artery. Fortunately, after the stent's placement, the artery remained open.

Because I received the stent, I was required to remain in the hospital overnight. It was also necessary that I begin taking an additional medication, the purpose of which is to prevent the formation of blood clots in and around that metal stent.

When Shirley, one of the coordinators, came to speak with me, I asked her about the narrowing of the coronary artery. "Why did that happen? Is it for the same reason I had narrowing of my original coronary arteries? Have I been doing something wrong?"

Her response was both encouraging and discouraging to me. She expressed some surprise and relief that it had taken eight years for the narrowing of the artery to occur. She told me that it often occurs after about five years following transplant surgery.

"What can I do to prevent future narrowing?"

Shirley replied: "It's really not anything you're doing or not doing. The immuno-suppressant medications you are taking cause narrowing in many patients' coronary arteries. Many transplant patients require stents after only five years, so you have done better than a great number.

"Also, a CMV infection will actually cause the coronary arteries to narrow. So just keep living your life and don't worry about changing anything."

I have had three CMV infections, so there have been three times that this second cause has combined with my twice-daily consumption of immuno-suppressive medications to bring about narrowing of one of my critically-important coronary arteries.

So the bad news is that I had a 90%-blocked coronary artery. The good news is that it was discovered and fixed before it caused a heart attack. The second bad news is that these blockages are caused by the very medications that are also keeping me alive by preventing my body from rejecting—and effectively killing—my transplanted heart. The very medications that are keeping me alive are also killing me! The second good news is that it took longer than normal for that much arterial narrowing to occur. The further bad news is that I can expect more of the same in the future. I was just recently informed that some heart transplant patients can receive as many as twelve stents! The further good news is that I will keep having annual exams so those additional, future blockages can be found and fixed. I believe that type of scenario is called "a mixed bag."

CHAPTER TWENTY-ONE

TRYING TO PREVENT CANCER

My face felt as though it was on fire.

As one ages, his life-long exposure to the sun usually causes dark spots to appear on his face, neck, hands and arms. This exposure to the sun causes skin cells to become abnormal. Abnormal cells, often referred to as pre-cancerous cells, tend to eventually become cancerous cells. Pre-cancerous spots develop, which need to be treated and/or removed by a dermatologist. This treatment and removal can continue to be necessary from the time a person is in his forties or fifties, for the rest of his life.

I have already written that my medications make cancer the likely number one cause of death for me to avoid. Being aware of that fact and since I had several pre-cancerous spots on my face, on January 4, 2013, I underwent several procedures to treat—and try to eliminate—those spots and to impede the development of new ones already on the way. So I went to the appointment I had set up more than a month earlier to have this work done. I timed the procedures to take place after the Christmas vacation, when I would have several weeks to recover without anyone but Dianne seeing me.

First, the doctor scraped off about 20 pre-cancerous spots on my face. Without pain medication, it was quite painful. Some were hard skin spots that were about 1/8-inch deep. After he finished that step, my face was a bloody mess all over. I had not known this would happen, so I had not taken anything for the pain.

He then washed my face and applied an acid chemical all over, including in the scraped-out spots. Then I came home for several hours to let the acid work and soak in.

Mid-afternoon, I returned and the doctor did what is called Intense Pulse Laser (IPL) treatment. The intense pulse is literally electric shocks all over my face and nose. Even with my eyes closed, I could see the red arc of the electrical current hitting my face. There were somewhere between 40 and 50 shocks. I involuntarily jumped with each shock. Two weeks later they said it was more painful than normal because of the scraped-off spots and the acid having been spread all over my face.

I was then taken into another room and placed on a stool with my face right next to red hot lights. (When I had been told about this procedure, I assumed it would be for 30 seconds, or so.) It went on and on. After a very long time, the assistant standing next to me, spraying water on my face, said, "You've done five minutes. Just fifteen minutes more!"

I really wondered if I could last another fifteen minutes. My face felt as though it was on fire.

When the twenty minutes were completed, I rode home in twenty-degree weather outside with the air conditioner on, blowing on my face, while I sprayed water on it every few seconds. At home, I reclined day and night with a fan blowing on my face and spraying water. Whenever I leaned forward or too far back, or stood up, it felt as though I was sticking my face into a furnace. Actually, the temperature of the air in the room was normal. It was my face that was that furnace-like temperature. I learned very quickly to spray my face immediately before standing up, and then to continue to spray it as I walked anywhere.

On days two to four, my face had become so swollen, my eyes were almost swollen closed. Dianne described my appearance as that of a burn victim. I am sure that actual burn victims have had to suffer experiences much worse than my voluntary ordeal. Nevertheless, my face went through the steps of swelling, blistering and bleeding of at least a mild to moderate burn. Every time, when I washed and dried my face as directed, it would start to bleed all over again. After a few days, I talked with the doctor and suggested that I not try to dry my face by using a paper towel to push against it and then peel the towel off. Each time, all the blisters would come off and multiple places on my face started bleeding all over again. I told the doctor that, because of the blood-thinning medication I must take, I would continue to re-start healing every day, and never get to day 2 of healing without starting all over again and again. He agreed with my proposal, that I should just let my face air dry. Finally, after more than a week, the blisters started coming off without new bleeding.

It took three weeks for my face to almost return to normal. It remained pink—initially dark pink—then progressively lighter over the next several weeks.

The only thing that made it worth doing these procedures was my hope that undergoing them would help lengthen my life. I had lived all of my life, including the eight and a half years since my transplant, having no cancer on my face because of exposure to the sun and side effects of my immune-suppressant medications. Perhaps—hopefully—if I could nearly start all over again, with no existing pre-cancerous spots, I should be able to last at least another eight plus years.

CHAPTER TWENTY-TWO

CONCLUSION

TO THIS BOOK,
NOT TO MY LIFE!

. . . I had a life-long dream fulfilled . . .

    In the nine years since my heart transplant, I have lived to see the remaining five of my six children marry. Most recently, when my daughter, Anne, was planning the date of her wedding to Samuel Inouye, she told Dianne that the only date Sam would we able to get several additional days of vacation from his medical residency would be to get married on my birthday. Dianne responded, "You can't get married on your dad's 60th birthday!"

Anne insisted it was the only day when they could have any honeymoon immediately after. Dianne told Anne she would ask me what I thought about having Anne's wedding on my birthday. When Dianne approached me with that idea, I responded, "I can't think of a better present for my birthday than having you and all of our children and their spouses in the temple with me!"

So Dianne and Anne proceeded to make arrangements for that date. (What I did not know was that Dianne already had scheduled a surprise 60th birthday party for me that day. But she did her magic and rescheduled it at noon on the day before. We then scheduled Anne's and Sam's wedding reception that same evening and their marriage in the temple on the following day—my birthday. It was a pleasure to welcome Sam into our family. On my 60th birthday, I had a life-long dream fulfilled of being in the temple with my wife and all of my children and all of their spouses.

I have now been blessed to see and get to know seventeen additional grandchildren—making a total of eighteen. In October, I will welcome number nineteen, as Anne gives birth to her first child. That means that since my successful transplant in 2004, I have been here for the marriages of the remaining five of my six children, and to welcome eighteen additional grandchildren who will have been born! That is almost too marvelous to believe.

Having these great blessings is wonderful to experience during this, my extended life. In addition to these great blessings, I have received so many more. I have been able to share countless experiences with my lovely and loving wife. She and I have been able to do hundreds of fun things with our children and their families. I am richly blessed.

I stated earlier that I had discussed with Dianne before our marriage how I wanted to travel to many different places. During my life—lives—I have been able to visit most of the states of our great country and over 40 different countries in the world. I have been on five of the seven continents. My work will possibly soon take me—and Dianne—to the sixth. I do not have any desire to go to Antarctica, so six will be wonderful and sufficient for me—us.

" . . . to help me learn dignity in suffering."

I bear witness that these blessings have come and do continue to come to me from a gracious and kind Lord. I express deep gratitude to Him, to my loving Father in Heaven, and to my wonderful family. My family is the primary reason for my wanting and fighting to live. I also express appreciation to my doctors, coordinators, nurses and all others who with them worked so hard and effectively to keep me alive and to help provide me with the opportunity to have a high quality of life. To so many kind and dear friends, I also express my hearts-felt thanks. (Pun intended.)

I look forward to the opportunity to live many more years with my dear wife, my children, my children-in-law, my grandchildren, my extended family and my friends and neighbors.

My life is wonderful. This life, given to me by the Great Creator, and preserved, restored and extended by Him, has been quite a journey. Many times and for extended periods of time, it has been extremely difficult. I still frequently have hard times. Each day, I experience negative and sometimes painful side effects from my years of illness, going through multiple steps of dying and from the powerful medications I must continue to take. I have daily muscle aches and pain. I have virtually daily neck aches, headaches, back, foot and leg aches and cramps. I grow fatigued much faster and more easily than I used to. I must stay out of the sunlight. I must be extremely careful about what I touch and who I am around. Each cold I have caught following my transplant has tended to last more than five weeks. I have come to realize that to a normal, healthy individual, the common cold's course is cut short by that person's immune system gaining control over the virus and then driving it out of the body. Having virtually no immune system, my body cannot drive the virus out of my body. I cannot take traditional medicines for cold, flu, congestion or pain. When I get something such as a cold or flu, I must simply let it run its course. Since my suppressed immune system cannot attack or fight off such illnesses, they simply take a long time to leave on their own. I often wonder for how much longer I will continue to have the blessing given me to live with my wife and family.

The above recitation of things I experience regularly, I note without complaint. They are much easier to handle than going through the process of slowly—or rapidly—dying. I experience so many good and great things that these are only minor inconveniences.

Through many trials, I have learned much. My patience has been tried and expanded. My faith has been tried and strengthened. My understanding of the Lord and of spiritual things has been greatly increased. My capacity to love has likewise grown. Unfortunately, I still need to further increase my patience, faith and relationship with God. To be able to live is a blessing, not a trial.

I strongly believe that in the pre-existence before I came to this Earth, I, along with everyone else who would be born into mortality, was given full disclosure by a loving Father in Heaven. He had set up as part of His great plan of salvation—His plan of happiness—the opportunity for every one of His spirit children to choose to come and have a mortal experience. This would give each person a physical body to combine with his or her spirit. It would also provide a time of testing, trials and learning. These would permit all mankind to prove whether or not they would be obedient and faithful to the Lord. These trials would also test everyone's patience and endurance. They would, in the process, allow each to become what he or she would choose to become. Through faith, obedience and striving to improve, each one would have the opportunity to become more and more as God is.

As part of the full disclosure given to all men and women—spirit children of God—we were told and shown much of what Earth life would be. We were thoroughly instructed. It is my belief that we were given opportunities to choose some of the experiences—even trials—we would have in mortality.

I remember saying early in our marriage, that I believe one of the choices I made in the pre-existence, was that I would be willing to have many serious and difficult health problems if my children would be good, upright and faithful people. I firmly believe that I was given both parts of that choice. I have experienced many years of extremely difficult and frightening health problems. Likewise, I have experienced the great joy of seeing each of my six children grow up in faith, obedience and goodness. They and my wife have been sources of great joy and love. They provided me with the seven great reasons for fighting so hard to continue to live. Since winning that fight on several occasions, with the blessings and miraculous interventions of the Lord, coupled with the gift of a borrowed heart from a wonderful person, they have continued to be a great source of joy and ample reward for those hard-fought battles.

Although the story that follows is not official doctrine, it teaches a principle in which I believe.

A man suffered from cystic fibrosis. He was a good and faithful man. One day, he asked the Lord why he had been cursed with such an awful disease. In answer, he was allowed to view himself in a classroom during the pre-existence. He told of his seeing a part of his pre-mortal experience and choices he made as he sat in that classroom for instruction in preparation for mortality. He wrote of an instructor during that pre-existence, teaching of ways to learn and progress during mortality. Apparently there are two basic ways to learn lessons—the slow way, having normal experiences, or a very quick way—through more disease and more severe pain. The man wrote of his instructor:

> He wrote on the board the words: "cystic fibrosis," and he turned and asked for volunteers. I was a volunteer; I saw me raise my hand and offer to take the challenge. The instructor looked at me and agreed to accept me.

> That . . . changed forever my perspective of the disease that I previously felt was a plague on my life. No longer did I consider myself a victim. Rather, I was a privileged participant, by choice, in an eternal plan. That plan, if I measured up to the potential of my choice, would allow me to advance in mortal life in the fastest way possible. . . . The specific choice of cystic fibrosis was to help me learn dignity in suffering. . . . I knew that I was a powerful, spiritual being that chose to have a short, but marvelous, mortal experience.

> . . . I found myself looking on . . . the Garden of Gethsemane. . . . I saw Christ undergoing his ordeal of pain with dignified endurance. . . . I understood that it was his choice, just as cystic fibrosis had been my choice. . . .[18]

In each of the years 1991, 2000 and 2004, and numerous times in every year in between and since, I was tempted to say, "Why me? Why is God doing this to me? Why must I be going through this, especially at my relatively young age? Why would He make my wife and children lose their husband and father?"

The fact is that God was NOT doing this to me. Why not me? Why should I be spared from suffering? How can I just expect to have things easy? Why should I be exempted from suffering, from trials or even from death?

Like everyone else, I came to Earth to receive a physical body, to prove myself to God and to work to become like He is. I believe that the Savior's command, "Be ye therefore perfect, as your Father which is in heaven is perfect,"[19] was intentional and serious. He really does expect us to seek to become more and more perfect, eventually having an opportunity, through His atoning sacrifice, to be able to continue the process after this life. If we have tried hard and sincerely enough during this mortal portion of our everlasting existence, we will be blessed to continue our progress hereafter. I must not let mortal trials and suffering keep me from faithfully pursuing the real purpose of my being here, and of the extension to that time I have received.

What I wrote in an earlier chapter bears repeating. I have repeatedly turned my thoughts to The Doctrine and Covenants, Section 122. There, the Lord speaks to the prophet while he is unlawfully incarcerated in a dingy, cold and filthy jail. God tells him of all of the types of tribulations that could befall him. He continues:

> And if thou shouldst be cast into the pit, or into the hands of murderers, and the sentence of death passed upon thee; if thou be cast into the deep; if the billowing surge conspire against thee; if fierce winds become thine enemy; if the heavens gather blackness, and all the elements combine to hedge up the way; and above all, if the very jaws of hell shall gape open the mouth wide after thee, know thou, my son, that all these things shall give thee experience, and shall be for thy good.

> The Son of Man hath descended below them all. Art thou greater than he?[20]

I have continued to remind myself that I am not greater.

Every time I wondered if I could take any more pain or worry—every time I was tempted to ask, "Why me?" or any other such questions—I rehearsed in my mind those passages of scripture and the great last two sentences. Every time, the response I repeated to myself was the same. "No, I am not greater than He." Then, re-examining myself and my suffering, I would always come to the same conclusion and determine again to have the same resolve to continue on faithful and obedient—trusting in a loving and merciful Lord. He could save me. "But if not," I was not going to succumb to the devil's continuous temptations to pity myself, to feel undeserving of my suffering and mistreated by the Lord. I chose to remain grateful to the Lord and for the blessings I had already received throughout my life.

It would continue to be my choice to remain a participant in an eternal plan. I hope I have learned to become more dignified in my suffering.

Many heroes

There are many heroes in the story of my receiving this second chance to live—this borrowed heart. I have spoken the truth about the Lord and His miraculous interventions in my life. Without

His repeatedly preserving and restoring my life, I would never have lived to receive my life-saving heart transplant.

My wife, my son and my daughters were amazing in their support—physically, emotionally and spiritually. They were my reasons for fighting with everything I could muster—physically, mentally, emotionally and spiritually—to live.

I will never be able to say enough about the care Dianne gave me, and how she stood with me through all of my trials. I know that second only to my own suffering was Dianne's suffering. She carried a heavy and hard load as she dealt with my suffering and tried to be positive and supportive.

On the card I gave Dianne on the first Valentine's Day following my transplant, among other things, I wrote, "You are the love of my lives!" She definitely is.

My children are sources of great joy and love for me.

My brothers and sisters: Joe, Lois, Ivan, Geniel, Jay, Carole, Ruby, Ray and John, have always been wonderful to me. My nieces and nephews are like great friends.

My extended family, friends and neighbors were so supportive and caring. They lifted our spirits and offered love and friendship during our frightening experiences. They joined their faith and prayers with ours in my behalf.

My cardiologist and other doctors, the transplant coordinators, physician's assistant, social worker, nurses, their assistants, and other medical people were so dedicated and professional, and yet so personable and caring. I cannot give adequate credit for their great work and friendship.

Certainly, my generous donor and her wonderful family were essential. Her willingness to be an organ donor not only saved my life, but also provided life-saving and life-improving organs and tissues to other strangers in great need. In the spirit world that follows mortality, I hope to tell her personally of my appreciation and respect.

May 2007 data from the United Network for Organ Sharing (UNOS) and the U.S. Department of Health and Human Services indicate that there were more than 96,000 people in the United States needing organ transplants, but very few donors. The difference between supply and demand of organs continues to increase dramatically. In 1995, the number of patients awaiting organs was 41,179. Only 19,369 (47%) received organs. By December, 2006, the waiting list had increased to 93,699, of which only 28,923 (31%) received transplants.[21]

Thousands of others in need of organ transplants to save their lives—64,776 (69%) in 2006—did not get what I was fortunate enough to receive. Many of those did not live to see 2007. Many of those who did were unable to make it to 2008. Those in need this year and in years to come will be hoping to be the beneficiary of some wonderful life-saving gift. This hope is tempered and made terribly solemn by the fact that in order for their life to be saved, someone else's will end. The one in need of a transplant does not cause or even wish the death of the donor. The donor's life would end whether life-saving organs were donated from that donor or not. That donor would die whether he or she was to be a lifesaver for others or not. The loving act at death that was planned for during the life of the donor will always be a legacy and memorial of each donor's goodness and charity.

EPILOGUE

A short time after I returned home with this new, borrowed heart, my neighbor called to ask me some spiritual questions. Having just gone through all that I had in the process of dying and receiving a life-saving heart transplant, I began my response to her question about what happens to a person who leaves mortality and moves to the spirit world, as follows: "When one dies—and stays dead . . ."

There will come a time when I will die—and stay dead. Sometime after that, I hope to have the opportunity to meet and thank my gracious donor.

Sometime thereafter, when I am resurrected, I will regain my original heart. It will be strong and healthy. It will have been made immortal through the grace, atonement and resurrecting power of the Lord Jesus Christ.

My borrowed heart—that gave me renewed life for many years—will return to its original owner's body, once again strong, healthy and immortal.

I know that I am living with a borrowed heart. I am also living on borrowed time. The fact is, we are all living on borrowed time. Some of you also have some other physical part that is borrowed. The loans we all receive come to us in the form of borrowed parts from the original owners. Ultimately, they come through the grace and mercy of the Master Lender/Broker. They tend to be in the form of borrowed grace—borrowed opportunities to change ourselves from being bad to being good. For some, they are opportunities to change from being good to becoming even better. In the end, if we use our borrowed time well, we may even be wise and become extremely good. That will put us well on our way on the loaned road to becoming as God is.

We will all continue to experience trials for as long as we live. Life never was intended to always be easy. How we deal with our trials will determine a number of things: (1) how happy or miserable we will choose to be. External conditions (external to our mind and spirit) do not dictate our internal level of happiness or dignity. We determine those. We choose to consider ourselves as victims of forces and events outside of our control, or as "privileged participants, by choice, in a glorious, eternal plan."[22] That plan was given by a loving, all-knowing, Father. It was set in place by a gracious Lord. They provided it to enable us to become powerful, spiritual beings, tried, proven and true.

I have learned that endurance is not just lasting through or putting up with trials with disgust or revulsion. Endurance is facing trials with patience, faith and a positive attitude. It is showing dignified acceptance of trials while we work to make ourselves better and more god-like. It is also experiencing spiritual growth amidst physical and/or emotional difficulties.

Anyone can be happy and pleasant when everything is going well. That does not require any particular character or strength. Being happy and pleasant when everything, or many things, are going poorly takes real character and faith. Doing that shows the true measure of a man or woman. The standard has been set by the Lord, Himself. If we expect to ever become as He is, or even close to it, the time to start seriously working on it is now.

I truly hope that you and I will put to good and wise use the borrowed time provided us by that great and loving Master.

My Main Reasons for Living

The following picture is already outdated, but still shows some of the extraordinary growth in my family and blessings since I received this borrowed heart.

FAMILY PORTRAIT TAKEN IN 2010

At the time of my heart transplant, only ten of the twenty-five in the above picture were part of my family. The twenty-five family members have since grown to thirty-two and will be thirty-three before the end of October 2013!

ABOUT THE AUTHOR

Glen W. Park and his wife, Dianne, have six children who are all married. They currently have eighteen grandchildren. One more is currently expected in 2013.

He is a businessman and attorney. He earned a B.A. in economics from the University of Utah and a Juris Doctorate from the University of Utah, College of Law. He has had executive involvement in a number of successful small businesses. In addition, he has practiced law for more than 37 years.

He has completed seven additional books. Four have already been published. The remaining three are now in the process of final reviews before publication. Several more are in various stages of completion.

Two related published books available at amazon.com are: *Our Next Life: A View Into The Spirit World;* and *What Satan Doesn't Want You To Know.*

SOURCES CITED

[1] The Doctrine and Covenants 6:22-24.

[2] St. Mark 10:29-30.

[3] Woodruff, Wilford, "Council Meetings Held Behind the Vail", (excerpts of Discourse delivered in Salt Lake City, Oct. 8, 1881.)

[4] Moroni 2:1-2.

[5] Moroni 3:2.

[6] See Daniel 3:13, 15.

[7] Daniel 3:16-18.

[8] 2 Corinthians 13:1.

[9] The Book of Revelation 3:20.

[10] *Ensign*, March 2004, The Church of Jesus Christ of Latter-day Saints, p. 31.

[11] See The Doctrine and Covenants, Section 122: 7-8.

[12] The Doctrine and Covenants, Section 122, part of verse 9.

[13] Op. cit., Daniel.

[14] Smith, Joseph F., *Gospel Doctrine*, 5th ed., Deseret Book Company, Inc., Salt Lake City, 1939, p. 436.

[15] Plumb, Charles, "Who Packs Your Parachute?", http://www.truthorfiction.com/rumors/p/parachute.htm.

[16] Barnard, Chistiaan, M. D., http://news.bbc.co.uk/2/hi/health/1470356.stm.

[17] *Teachings of Presidents of the Church: Wilford Woodruff*, The Church of Jesus Christ of Latter-day Saints, Salt Lake City, 2004, p. 77.

[18] Gibson, Arvin S., *Journeys Beyond Life—True Accounts of Next-world Experiences*, Bountiful, Horizon Publishers, 1994, pp. 187-190.

[19] St. Matthew 6:48.

[20] The Doctrine and Covenants, Section 122, part of verse 7 and all of verse 8.

[21] See data from United Network for Organ Sharing (UNOS) and the U.S. Department of Health and Human Services, May 2007.

[22] Gibson, op. cit.

25531771R00117

Made in the USA
Charleston, SC
06 January 2014